KINGSLEY L. DENNIS, researcher, and writer. I the Sociology Department at Lancaster University, UK. Kingsley is the author of numerous articles on social futures, technology and new media communications, global affairs, and conscious evolution. He is the author of several critically acclaimed books including *The Sacred Revival*, *The Phoenix Generation*, *New Consciousness for a New World*, *Struggle for Your Mind*, *After the Car*, and the celebrated *Dawn of the Akashic Age* (with Ervin Laszlo). He has travelled extensively and lived in various countries. He currently lives in Andalusia, Spain. His homepage is www.kingsleydennis.com

HEALING THE WOUNDED MIND

THE PSYCHOSIS OF THE MODERN WORLD AND THE SEARCH FOR THE SELF

KINGSLEY L. DENNIS

CLAIRVIEW

Clairview Books Ltd.,
Russet, Sandy Lane,
West Hoathly,
W. Sussex RH19 4QQ

www.clairviewbooks.com

Published by Clairview Books 2019

A CIP catalogue record for this book is available from the British Library

ISBN 978 1 912992 04 1

Cover by Morgan Creative incorporating artwork © vectorpouch/Freepik
Typeset by DP Photosetting, Neath, West Glamorgan
Printed and bound by 4Edge Ltd, Essex

Contents

Foreword

In his new book Kingsley Dennis addresses the greatest question we can ask about our life on this planet. Is there a future for our life on Earth? We have created conditions that place in question the continuation of all life on the planet. We do not seem to recognize this and to take it seriously. We are experiencing a 'metaphysical malaise' where everything that transcends our immediate preoccupations is removed from our view. It is as if a magician would hide from us the reality we need to apprehend if we are to live on Earth.

Kingsley asked me to discuss the origins of this malaise and its possible cure, and to formulate what he calls 'a rallying call'. This is a major challenge: a question, with an important but not readily discoverable answer. On these pages I try to contribute to its clarification by exploring the nature of the problems that confront us in the world.

The malaise Kingsley has in mind is real; it can be felt in every breath we take. I suggest that while its manifestation is metaphysical, the malaise stems from the way we live on this planet and the way our thinking patterns are influenced.

The problem is what we do to ourselves as well as to the planet. We use sophisticated technologies of energy and information to satisfy our wants. Using these technologies has resulted in extinguishing fifty percent of the wildlife in the biosphere. We have the power to extinguish all higher forms of life with the push of a button. The fact is that we have become a danger to all forms of life, including our own. Why did this turn of events come about? Does it make us happier, more fulfilled? According to all current indications, far from it. Protests and frustrations are becoming a daily occurrence, and they are becoming more violent. Large masses are suffering from depression, and more and more individuals are indulging in mindless acts of violence. A sea of hapless and helpless humans is roaming the planet in search of a place to live – or just to survive.

The way we are now in the world is not a good way to be, but it is not necessarily the way we need to be. We have the means and the know-how to live on Earth without lacking the resources needed for a healthy existence. Yet, why have we become a scourge?

The first thing to realize is that whatever went wrong, did not go wrong for the whole of humankind. The great majority of humans inhabiting the planet are not creators of today's problems, but their victims. Given a chance, most people would live on Earth without destroying each other and the environment. As Aristotle noted, man is a social animal. We are not intrinsically violent and destructive.

The very fact that we could survive as a species for some five million years and could maintain ourselves as a conscious cultural species for about fifty thousand is evidence that basic human nature is not the problem. It is not the bulk of the human population that is responsible for becoming a scourge, only a segment of it. The question is, why did a segment of humankind create unsustainable and now critical conditions for itself, for the rest of humanity, and for all life in the biosphere?

The plausible answer is that humanity became a scourge without conscious intention. This was a side-effect of the unreflective aspiration not just to maintain, but to constantly increase our wealth and power. Seeking to increase wealth and power by a segment of the population by using the means available for it, turned out to depress the chances of acquiring and maintaining viable levels of wealth and power for the rest.

For millennia, people in all walks of life and in all parts of the world have been pursuing the tasks of everyday existence without killing each other and their neighbours. The fact that humanity could survive and spread over the habitable regions of the planet suggests that being a scourge is not its natural condition. Something happened that subverted the healthy instincts of this species and replaced them with impulses and aspirations that threaten the continuation of life on Earth. What has happened?

A witty but insightful remark by Mark Twain points to the

answer. For a young boy with a new hammer, he said, the whole world seems like a nail. Hammering away at the world may be well-intentioned – it's a natural impetus to use the power we have in our hand – but it can create unforeseen and highly dangerous conditions.

Mark Twain has 'hit the nail on its head'. We act as a child who hammers away beyond the need for it and beyond its utility. We are like children in a candy store or in toy shop. We eat until we become sick and use our toys without regard for the effect that has on others.

The technologies of the modern age are a 'super-hammer' that transforms the world into a worldwide candy-store and toy-shop. We indulge ourselves with candy and toys regardless of our real needs – and without taking seriously the effect on others. We release vast energies in nature and use them to power the systems that indulge us. We channel the flow of electrons in integrated circuits in ways that they transmit information for our systems. We play in the global toy-shop without adequate regard for the effect on others.

This is a risky way to behave. Energy and information are fundamental elements in the world. In the last count we, and all systems around us, are configurations of energy and information. It turned out that energy can be accessed and used to create conditions that went beyond our wildest dreams. It turned out that information can be likewise channelled and manipulated with mind-boggling results. The nuclear bomb and the nuclear power station on the one hand, and the computer and the internet on the other, are clear examples.

Can we blame those who can access the new energy- and information-toys for using them to increase their wealth and power? We cannot blame them any more than we can blame a child for hitting with his new hammer, and a child for wanting more candy and new toys. The human species is not evil, just naïve and self-centred. Now the time for acting with the self-centred naiveite of a child is over. The harm that results from it could affect all people and endanger all life.

The malaise we feel is more than metaphysical: it has grounds in the real world. We have created these grounds ourselves, even if we created them inadvertently. The way to heal ourselves, heal humanity, and heal the planet is not to assign blame, but to wake up and assume responsibility. We cannot survive on this planet without acting in recognition of the consequences of our actions.

Recognizing the root causes of the malaise Kingsley is writing about is the first step. It is a crucial step, and I hope that the readers of this brilliant and profound book will recognize the urgency of taking it. For all of us, inhabitants of this precious and endangered planet, the time has come to grow up.

Ervin Laszlo
December 2018

Introduction

What's Going On?

Mother, mother
There's too many of you crying
Brother, brother, brother
There's far too many of you dying
You know we've got to find a way
To bring some lovin' here today

Marvin Gaye
What's Going On

Isn't there something fundamentally wrong with how the world is right now? Don't you see it — *feel* it? We are a species with noble character, with a great spirit, and with a sacred soul. In our hearts we wish only for the betterment of all people; for love and justice and communion. And yet what we see going on in the world is nothing less than complete madness. We have to say it exactly as it is — there is a sickness going on and this pathogen is being perpetrated on a vast scale.

We live in a world where economic greed overrides all other factors. Nations, corporations, and individuals commit horrendous acts that include impoverishment, deprivation, psychological and physical torture, and even murder, just for financial gain. Nations, groups, and individuals behave horrendously toward others; there is constant bullying and harassment upon all social and cultural levels. Violence is endemic across the globe, at all levels. Pharmaceutical corporations would rather turn a profit than support health and well-being. Governmental bodies and agents participate in drug trafficking on a huge scale in order both to make money and promote addiction amongst the masses. Rich individuals and corporations hide their money through illegal offshore schemes rather than contribute to the welfare of their communities. People in high office consistently abuse, harass, and violate people within their power as a sign of their high status. The health of the planet and its natural environment is constantly mistreated and polluted; again, mostly for the sake of economic gain. And the list goes on.

We have entered the third millennium and we pride ourselves on being an inventive and intelligent species. We have probed off-planet and have allegedly placed people on the moon. We are now planning trips further afield into the solar system and having people live on the planet Mars. We are an incredibly creative and compassionate species. So, what is wrong? Why do so many people, so much of the time, adhere to thinking and ways of behaviour that is nothing short of insanity? Why do we live in a topsy-turvy, upside-down reality?

The reason, I propose, is that we are not living within *our right minds*. And with this book it is my intention to explore how we might have 'lost' our minds to a collective psychosis that seeks to imbue us with a traumatic mind. This is no flight of fantasy. There are indeed indigenous and wisdom teachings that tell of a mental force that exists in the collective consciousness field that came to usurp our minds. Various traditions refer to these nefarious mindsets as *wetiko, predators, archons, Ahriman, the flyers,* and more. In these pages I shall discuss some of these traditions and what they say about how this 'alien mind' has entrapped and traumatized the human collective mind. At the same time, notwithstanding the perspectives of these various traditions, we have modern depth psychology that speaks of the human collective unconscious.

Another side of this story is that, as a global species, we are also projecting the wounds of our collective unconscious out into the world. This is both a traumatic and cathartic process. It needs to be done if we are to cleanse ourselves to be ready for the global transition at hand. And there is no doubt about it that we are in the midst of a great, historical transition.

As I have written about in several of my previous books, we have entered a period of profound transformation and transition. We are quite literally shifting from one historical epoch to another. And this transition has been, relatively speaking, extremely rapid. In order to prepare ourselves for a new planetary civilization that is to come into existence, we need first to cleanse ourselves of our collective unconscious traumas and of the shadows that lurk in the dark recesses of our minds. This book is about recognizing those mental shadows as well as the inherent need for meaning and genuine selfhood within our everyday existence.

This book is about these two issues: the seeming madness of the modern world, and the need to find meaning within it. In all cultures, at all times, connections to the transcendental exist. We have to keep that thread going. This book is unlike any other book I have written – and it was a difficult book to write.[*] The fact is, this book *didn't want to be written.* Yes, that's it; the book rebelled against being made flesh. It pushed against me physically, mentally, and spiritually. I had to force this book into birth – it was a difficult labour. It may also be a difficult read. The Wounded Mind did not wish to be known. It did not wish to be recognized, identified, or named. There were many times where I questioned my own reasons for writing this book; and more so for ever wishing it to be public. Yet in the end I also rebelled. I pushed back against this incorrigible force and remained persistent throughout. Why? Because I agree with what was written in the Gnostic Gospel of Philip – 'So long as the root of wickedness is hidden, it is strong. But when it is recognized, it is dissolved. When it is revealed, it perishes... It is powerful because we have not recognized it.' If we ignore such things, they do not go away – on the contrary, they grow stronger through our unawareness. It is because I regard recognition of the Wounded Mind to be that important, I have decided to write this book. Do not be dismayed as you read – feel empowered.

In order to be healed we first need to be aware of what ails us. We need to become alert to the situation we find ourselves in. To go forward in the best possible manner means we walk ahead with full, open eyes. This book is about opening those eyes and beginning the search for genuine meaning and liberty in our lives. Let's walk – heads up!

---

[*]Perhaps the only other book that comes close is *The Struggle for your Mind: Conscious Evolution & the Battle to Control How We Think* (Inner Traditions, 2012).

Part One

OUT OF OUR MINDS

In Part One of the book I outline what I call the 'magician's trick' and how this spell has rendered us docile and vulnerable to an invasion of our minds. Our mental and psychological states have been susceptible to a form of psychosis that I have called the 'Wounded Mind'. In the following chapters I explain how this mental pathogen manifests and how it has been a part of our cultural conditioning from childhood.

Chapter One

The Magician's Trick

'... in the darkness charlatans are easily mistaken for sages.'

Chantal Delsol

'Against whom shall we do battle, where shall we direct our attack, when the very breath in our lungs is impregnated with the same injustice that haunts our thinking and holds the stars in stupefaction?'

Emile Cioran, *A Short History of Decay*

There was once a Magician who built his house near a large and prosperous village. One day he invited all the people of the village to dinner. 'Before we eat,' he said, 'we have some entertainments.'

Everyone was pleased, and the Magician provided a wonderful magic show, with card tricks, illusions, animals appearing from nowhere, and one thing turning into another. The people were delighted. Then the Magician asked: 'Would you like dinner now, or more entertainments?'

Everyone called for more entertainments, for they had never seen such a show before. They had seen shows on television, yet nothing was as exciting as this. So, the Magician continued amazing the people with his illusions and fantastic trickeries. The people went wild with excitement.

He asked them again, and they wanted more. Again, the Magician gave them more entertainments. Then he asked them if they wanted to eat, and they said that they did. So the Magician made them feel that they were eating, diverting their attention with a number of tricks, through his magical powers.

The imaginary eating and entertainments went on all night. When it was dawn, some of the people said, 'We must go to work.' So the Magician made those people imagine that they went home, got ready for work, and actually did a day's work.

In short, whenever anyone said that he had to do something, the Magician made him think first that he was going to do it, then, that he had done it and finally that he had come back to the Magician's house.

Finally, the Magician had woven such spells over the people of the village that they worked only for him while they thought that they were carrying on with their ordinary lives. Whenever they felt a little restless he made them think that they were back at dinner at his house, and this gave them pleasure and made them forget.

And what happened to the Magician and the people, in the end? Do you know, I cannot tell you, because he is still busily doing it, and the people are still largely under his spell.

Life in modern societies is much like this tale of the magician's dinner. We have been hypnotized into believing that we are engaging in useful, everyday tasks when in actual fact we are duped into performing tasks for a system that neither truly benefits us nor has our well-being at heart. Krishnamurti famously said that 'It is *no measure* of health to be well adjusted to a profoundly sick society.' As this poignant and startling phrase suggests, we are living within a 'sick', or rather wounded, modern society – and we are in need of deep healing.

As I shall explore throughout this book, we have a psychic malaise that has corrupted our collective mind, which keeps many of us unaware or 'asleep' to our true predicament. And this true predicament is that many of us continue to work for the Magician. By working for the Magician we neglect our true *self* and its connection to a great inheritance of honourable values, wisdom, and compassion. Humanity is a noble species that is trying, step by step, to grow, develop, learn, and understand its way and place within its current reality. As a species we have the power to dream and manifest a wondrous world into being. We can nurture relations and friendship with our fellow creatures, and with our natural environments. We can practice loving compassion, forgiveness, understanding, and empathy for all living and non-living entities that share our reality. There are many instances where humans have shown, and continue to show, this incredible capacity. And so, we must ask: why is humanity suffering so much? Why have so many of us neglected our contract to be honourable custodians alongside other living creatures? Why have we been so cruel to our fellow human beings?

As a young man in my teens, I was an avid reader of poetry. A line from the English poet Philip Larkin has always stayed with me. It is taken from his poem 'This Be The Verse' and it goes —

> Man hands on misery to man.
> It deepens like a coastal shelf.

I have always asked myself — why do we keep handing on our misery? What's happened to us? Something must have gotten into our minds?

I wish to explore this question further. In fact, this question — *what has gotten into our minds?* — is the very thesis of this book. As I shall examine in more detail in the next chapter, we may be participants to a mental 'collective invasion'. Sound fantastical? Well, something unruly and odd is certainly going on within our species. Something has affected/infected our collective humanity. Wouldn't you agree?

As Shakespeare says in his bloody play *Macbeth* — 'Fair is foul, and foul is fair.'[*] Our fairness has been turned foul by the Magician's spell, and the result is that so many of us are unhappy, dissatisfied, frustrated, anxious, and so on. Why is it that so many people in our modern societies are seemingly dissatisfied when they have acquired most things to keep them happy? Perhaps a society that provides superficial comfort produces conditions that do not develop people or cause them to turn an inward gaze or to question notions of their meaning and existence. Too long a time cushioned by material comforts has produced only a superficial form of happiness, where people cling to routine for security and fiercely protect their small advantages.

We must face the fact that there are no instruction sets for how to live a human life. No one ever placed a tablet in our hands at an early age and told us that here were the secrets to living a meaningful life. In past eras our societies had various religious structures to promote a faith-based life where hard toil guaranteed a decent afterlife for the humble. And now these orthodox religious struc-

---

[*] Act I, Scene 1.

tures have largely fallen into their own materialistic powerhouses of power, control, and greed. Their responses to our contemporary questions are woefully lacking, and many of their representatives have no inkling of the true needs of the time. We've had to reach a point of obvious spiritual disarray – of gyrating gurus and wealthy cult personalities – before we bear witness within us to the great lack that hungers us. We must wonder why so many people are content to live their lives without apparent meaning; or to even question why they live or why they die.

We must also question why it is that our modern cultures promote entertainments that manipulate and play upon excessively distorted images of mental and emotional anguish as well as exaggerated portrayals of sexuality. We are bombarded daily with images of death. In fact, a recent study into Western media announced that the most repeated word in media is 'death'. The study revealed that in the first twelve years of a child's life, they would have been subjected to around 20,000 murders through television news and programmes, films, online content, and video games.[1] These forms of stimulation directly target a person's mental, emotional, and physical states, which in turn hampers the operation of more harmonious and necessary developmental energies. Our contemporary behaviour is now centred around emotion in a way that allows people to be entertained as well as manipulated on an unprecedented level. For so many of us, we live in a world of increasing signs and symbols yet of decreasing meaning. The meaning we try to ascribe to the symbols that constitute our daily lives may give us superficial or short-term comfort, yet they largely fail to provide for long-term vision or lasting hope.

It is unfortunate that the meaning of life is often a meaningless question to so many people. Many of us are forced to live our lives trying to make this lack of meaning palatable by finding smaller meanings for ourselves; such as through work, family, social status, and conventions of 'success'. Seeking that which is transcendent – the 'unnameable' – might sound like madness to many people, and certainly there is little place for it in modern societies that prize themselves on progress. And yet a life that seeks meaning is its own adventure. A life that is filled with meaningless activities leaves no significant traces – it is a life that has lost its connection. As the thirteenth century Persian poet Rumi said:

> There is one thing in this world you must never forget to do. If you forget everything else and not this, there's nothing to worry about, but if you remember everything else and forget this, then you will have done nothing in your life.

What Rumi is suggesting is that we each have a connection with the 'unnameable' that does not need to be named, but it does require to be recognized internally and dealt with. Yet perhaps too many of us are waiting for something to happen; for something to compel us into action – into awakening. And in the meantime, our societies slumber and our institutions force this cultural inertia into our receptive minds.

It is as if we are still waiting on a large, empty stage for Godot to appear to us; perhaps as a hologram, or through our augmented reality devices and our virtual reality headsets. Where is this Godot? Where is Hermes the eternal trickster? Modernity has tried hard to convince us that we are at home in the world, and that all its trappings are natural to us. As if waiting for Godot, we should be content to continue conversing between ourselves, regardless of whether anyone is listening. Our increasingly complex world is presented in an overly simplified and conformist way. We don't need wisdom to understand the world, we only need to know how to use Twitter to express a few letters.

Modernity has also given us the perspective that anything that is important lays external to us. We are just flesh and bone, and bits of matter to be modified and tampered with. The attitude of the 'modern mindset' to the external world has largely been one of hostility – we have been conquering the external world for the greater part of recent history, instead of mastering our own inner nature. This hostile attitude ignores the reality that all life is inter-dependent and that our lives are a projection of our inner realities – that is, our fears, anxieties, and insecurities become projected into the world the same as our hopes, visions, and dreams. Whatever we project externally eventually, becomes our sense of reality. And this is precisely the matter I allude to throughout these pages. If we have inherited a corrupted collective mind, then we are projecting a tarnished collective reality. We have quite literally been mis-programmed and we are living through this bad screenplay. Again, quoting the great bard Shakespeare – 'All the world's a stage/And all the men and women merely players/They have their exits and their entrances/And one man in his time plays many parts.'[*]

It is important to recognize that we all share a collective reality, despite our cultural differences. Although it alters depending upon where we were born and in which cultures we live, the methods each modern system uses are basically the same – we are provided with beliefs, cultural references, and norms and attitudes. The writer Doris Lessing referred to this as 'The prisons *we choose* to live inside.'[†] And within these psychological prisons many people, as well as the institutions of the modern world, have rejected the wisdom of sages, mystics, philosophers, and even the voices of creative artists. They prefer instead the superficial trappings, entertainments, and technological distractions of the consumerist marketplace. Now, I wish to be clear here – I am not anti-tech-nology. In fact, I am a great supporter of it; but not at the expense of the human vision. Despite the technological progress of the external world, there must always be a developed interior world to observe, reflect, and to question it. Without this, the exterior life is unleashed without values. Without an interior life to seek for significance, what gives meaning to our lives? It is essential in life to reflect upon and examine the human condition.

The Human Condition in Modern Times

Modern life has attempted to reinterpret the human condition. It wishes to see it as an external drive for progress, and this has resulted in a separation from our need to seek for essential inner

---

[*] From *As You Like It* (Act II, Scene VII).

[†] See Doris Lessing's *Prisons We Choose to Live Inside* (originally published in 1986).

meaning in our lives. This modern 'project' has sought to divorce the human being from our imperative to find our *essential self*. The human project, if we wish to call it that, can never be 'completed' — it is an eternal quest to always be *becoming*. The Sufi master Tariqavi is quoted as saying,

> When you have found yourself you can have knowledge. Until then you can only have opinions. Opinions are based on habit and what you conceive to be convenient to you. The study of the Interior Life requires self-encounter along the way. You have not met yourself yet. The only advantage of meeting others in the meantime is that one of them may present you to yourself. Before you do that, you will possibly imagine that you have met yourself many times. But the truth is that when you do meet yourself, you come into a permanent endowment and bequest of knowledge that is like no other experience on earth.[2]

What we are truly seeking for when we are in our 'right minds' is power over ourselves — not for power over others. It is clear then that the world is in need of soulful healing, rather than wanting to acquire greater power through corrupt and manipulative means. The world requires healed, integrated, and balanced people; for that which we lack in ourselves we shall always find lacking in the world outside. If we are not happy within ourselves, the world will not appear a happy place to us.

It is a common situation that we tell other people we are happy when for much of the time we are not. We buy more and more items to feel happiness within ourselves or to buy happiness in others. Many people in modern cultures continue to accumulate goods and possessions whilst feeling empty within. Such consumerism empties our pockets but fails to fill our souls. And not only our physical lives become crowded with belongings but our psychological spaces too. We are crowded with those belongings that have accumulated as psychological attachments: the beliefs, ideologies, nationalisms, opinions, likes, dislikes, and all the rest. We are often cluttered in our minds by belonging to *this* and *that* and all the other things that we cling to or that cling to us. And this is where some of the trauma is situated, because our belongings are now breaking apart. As our social, cultural, economic, and work lives go through change and transformation – as they are currently doing – then the clinging to old 'belongings' will only serve to cause greater disorientation and internal dislocation.

It feels as if for much of the time we are just getting by through covering over our doubts with other issues; and yet these doubts are shared globally and not just individually. In fact, they are endemic within modern societies. Rather than seeking the *essential*, we allow ourselves to indulge in wanting to live with more comfort, with greater ease, and with less effort. And yet we are creating ever more contradictions and paradoxes for ourselves, as we get drawn in ever deeper into the Magician's spell. Our lack of any coherent understanding will likely morph into extremisms and fanaticisms that come to plague us. Already it seems as if we are living in a world that is displaying increasing outward signs of craziness and psychopathic tendencies. We must ensure that the world never has more critics than visionaries, or more complainers than positive doers. It is essential that no matter how much trauma is projected into our external reality, we do not lose sight of our frameworks of personal meaning.

Pre-modern societies, for example, lived within their own frameworks of meaning. Not all questions had their answers, yet mysteries and the mysterious at least had a home in which they could exist. We often live today within an atmosphere of meaningless questions and contradictory answers. The pursuit of meaning has been replaced by the pursuit of progress. Progress may alleviate some of our suffering and pains, yet it shall never compensate for the lack of fulfilment we feel inside, for this requires metaphysical or transcendental nourishment. Any notion of the spiritual, or the metaphysical, is often considered inessential to our daily life, and we are taught to dismiss it. Modernity's task was thus seen as freeing us from the illusions of transcendence. And yet the desire, or the need, for some Absolute remains deep within us and can never be totally eradicated. Perhaps it is this contradiction that lies at the heart of our contemporary distress.

Modern life also tries to eradicate, or at least hide, all sense of enigma. Yet it is precisely these enigmas that make our lives rich in wonder and awe. To attempt to abolish them is an act of great ignorance and hubris. Unanswerable questions should be embraced and not rejected. Mystery and the mysterious should be allowed a space to thrive and enthral us. It is this sense of mystery that keeps us curious, and curiosity is one of our driving, motivating forces. And yet mystery, it seems, has been abolished by the arrival of the more 'sophisticated' mind. Modern societies may well praise their sophisticated intellectual culture, yet it comes at the cost of having a deteriorated spiritual culture. As French philosopher Chantal Delsol says,

> And so we find in our societies a very sophisticated intellectual culture and a very poor spiritual culture. For anything concerned with the soul is considered not incommunicable, but *dangerous* to communicate... Ultimately, the attention paid to life's mysteries is diluted because they are kept out of sight.[3]

Delsol makes an important point here; namely, that which belongs to the experience of the human soul is considered not only incommunicable, but rather *dangerous* to communicate. In the end, life's mysteries are kept out of sight because they cannot fully be known and thus controlled. There is a spell upon us, and we are being distracted from the *essential*. Here is a tale to consider:

> A lion was captured and imprisoned in a reserve where, to his surprise, he found other lions that had been there for many years, some even their whole life, having been born in captivity. The newcomer soon became familiar with the activities of the other lions and observed how they were arranged in different groups.
>
> One group was dedicated to socializing, another to show business, whilst yet another group was focused on preserving the customs, culture and history from the time the lions were free. There were church groups and others that had attracted the literary or artistic talent. There were also revolutionaries who devoted themselves to plot against their captors and against other revolutionary groups. Occasionally, a riot broke out and one group was removed or killed all the camp guards, so that they had to be replaced by another set of

guards. However, the newcomer also noticed the presence of a lion that always seemed to be asleep. He did not belong to any group and was oblivious to them all. This lion appeared to arouse both admiration and hostility from the others. One day the newcomer approached this solitary lion and asked him which group he belonged to.

'Do not join any group,' said the lion. 'Those poor ones deal with everything but the essential.'

'And what is essential?' asked the newcomer.

'It is essential to study the nature of the fence.'

A whole society can be distracted. There is a pertinent analogy here to how, in 256 AD, the Persian army took Antioch from the Roman Empire. Many of the inhabitants were attending the roman theatre and were oblivious to the enemy archers who had climbed up behind them into the stands. The actors down below had seen the enemy archers and were desperately trying to warn them with hand signals. But the audience did not understand, thinking it part of the entertainment – until it was too late. They were amused up to the point of death. Perhaps we too, in the words of social critic Neil Postman, are 'amusing ourselves to death'.[4]

It appears that our human condition is being increasingly bombarded by the impacts of our modern, technologically-driven lives. Perhaps for many of us this is traumatic enough. There is little wonder then why so many people are addicted to a life of high stimulation, which by its very nature also creates anxiety. Many people are forced, or seduced, into lives that are continually stressful and busy. There is no room for the spaces, the intervals, of internal reflection. Yet similar to how music is not music without the intervals, so life is not a life without those internal spaces.

There are many external forces in the world that are trying to make us live, not according to our own sense but according to dominant social narratives – what I call the dominant 'Social Mind'. We are told that we must live according to certain social narratives that generally benefit those systems that have no interest in the human soul. And when we deny ourselves such essential nutrients, we find that we have a discomfort within us. People are taking increasing amounts of anti-depressants, or stimulants, as well as relaxants – we take drugs to bring us up and other drugs to take us down. Again, this is all part of the illusion of the Magician's spell. Yet how did this all come about in the first place? Just what is this spell, and why does it appear that so many of us are collectively acting insane? In other words – *what has gotten into our minds?*

This is exactly what we are going to address.

Chapter Two

An Invasion of the Collective Mind

'Greed knows no limits.
Perversion knows no borders.
Arrogance knows no frontiers
Deceit knows no edges.
These characteristics all tend to push towards an extreme,
always moving forward once the initial infection sets in.'

Jack Forbes

The question we are confronted with is a collective one, and it concerns us all. Why are so many of us, our fellow humans, behaving so badly? And not only badly, but in a way that is detrimental to our own well-being. It would seem more than strange, verging on the insane, that any creature would wish deliberately to harm its own environment and support systems. Yet for us humans we have the significant added factor of being conscious of our actions, and self-conscious in our reflective understanding. So, again, we ask – *what has gotten into our minds?*

It appears that this question has been asked many times in the past, over and over, by many thinkers, philosophers, sages, and mystics. It is a question that has concerned a great number of people for a long time. And yet I suspect that the issue is of great concern today because for the first time in our human history we are behaving as a global species. Many of us physically move around the world, whether willingly – travellers, adventurers, and tourists – or through forced migration. We have access to international media and entertainment through our televisions (cable and satellite) as well as through the internet. And with our communication technologies we are sharing our ideas, stories, opinions, and the rest, all across the wide world. We can know almost instantly some news from a far-flung corner of the world.

And so it is as if we are mixing and morphing together as a collective. At this time in our human history, a negative infection of our collective mindset would be disastrous.

In this chapter I shall consider the hypothesis that a mental infection (a psychosis) has entered the collective human mindset; that is, into our collective consciousness – or, as Jung would say, into our collective unconscious. I shall examine this proposition from four different cultural contexts: indigenous Native American, Western psychology, Central American shamanism, and European theosophy. And I shall give it my own name – the *Wounded Mind*. First, I turn to the indigenous Native American tradition.

Wetiko

Jack Forbes, a Native American scholar and activist, has long considered the question of what has gotten into the human mind – and came up with an answer for it. After long study he came to the conclusion that humanity is suffering from a specific disease, a psychosis:

> For several thousands of years human beings have suffered from a plague, a disease worse than leprosy, a sickness worse than malaria, a malady much more terrible than smallpox ... I call it *cannibalism* ... But whatever we call it, this disease, this *wetiko* (cannibal) psychosis, is the greatest epidemic sickness known to man.[1]

Cannibalism, *wetiko* – what is he referring to? In Forbes' view, he defines cannibalism as the act of consuming another person's life for one's own private purpose or profit. This is of course different from actually physically eating a person, yet it's still an act of consumption, or devouring. And *wetiko*? It turns out that *wetiko* is a Cree term (*windigo* in Ojibway, *wintiko* in Powhatan) that refers to an evil person or spirit which terrorizes other creatures by means of terrible acts. And in Forbes' view, the great tragedy of humankind is that our history for the past two thousand years has largely been a tale of the psychosis of the 'wetiko disease' as he calls it. He goes as far back as to include the Egyptians, Babylonians, and Assyrians as cultures that helped to spread the *wetiko* disease throughout the Middle East. Afterwards, it was the Macedonians and Greeks under Alexander who spread it still further until it finally landed in the lap of the Roman Empire who, according to Forbes, really expanded the *wetiko* infection. What he is saying here is that this psychosis is a particular mindset that took form as certain hierarchical cultures and civilizations began to grow. And in order to maintain control, power, and to further bloody expansion, this mindset was deliberately cultivated, encouraged, and then developed as the dominant perspective and narrative. In fact, it was a crucial perspective that had to be propagated in order to maintain all status quo power structures within a developing culture. To not adhere to this specific mindset almost certainly meant annihilation and eradication in the face of other competing cultures (as was the case with Forbes' inherited Native American ancestral cultures).

For the last two thousand years then, at least, the world has been witnessing the growth and expansion of a particular kind of mindset. And this has been inherited from culture to culture, almost in the same way we pass on the DNA in our genes. The *wetiko* disease is principally an infectious meme that has embedded itself into the very DNA of human civilization. Forbes recognized this for he considered that the development of the *wetiko* disease corresponded exactly to the rise of what came to be called 'civilization'. Forbes knew that this was no mere coincidence as the history of humanity has been about the rise and fall of 'great' empires and authoritarian societies which fill our history books. And, as Forbes says, it is exactly these types of societies that are *wetiko*. As he clearly states:

> ...the heroes of the history textbooks, are usually imperialists, butchers, founders of authoritarian regimes, exploiters of the poor, liars, cheats and torturers. What that means is that the *wetiko* disease has so corrupted European thinking (at least of the ruling groups) *that wetiko behaviour and wetiko goals are regarded as the very fabric of European evolution.*[2]

According to Forbes, the very idea of civilization incorporates a collective of persons who consider it necessary to perform evil,

violent, and dishonest acts in order to maintain the power structures of their society. Also, in order for the ruling few to maintain
stable power and order, they must convince, persuade, or condition
the masses within their society/civilization to either believe and
support the same, or at the very least not to rebel against it. The
functioning of our modern societies has been derived from this
operation of providing a dominant mindset — or social narrative —
and manipulating its collective consent through coercion (the past)
or persuasive propaganda (the present). Of course, our societies
also require a substantial number of law enforcers — police, soldiers, and other armed forces of control — to maintain physical
order in times of civil disruption or unrest.

Forbes considers that the stronger the sense of a coherent,
modern, and rational-material civilization or society, the more
apparent and palpable is the presence of *wetiko* behaviour. This is
especially the case in terms of European history, according to
Forbes:

> European history is replete with almost continuous examples of
> human depravity — epoch after epoch of imperialistic wars, frequent
> examples of the systematic murdering of followers of different reli-
> gions or members of different ethnic groups, almost continuous
> campaigns to liquidate or forcibly assimilate this or that nationality,
> rigid systems of class exploitation, the brutal subjection of peasants,
> slaves and workers and, finally, literally thousands of examples of
> lying, deceit, poisoning, duplicity, torture and sadism, ranging from
> the murders of Byzantine monarchs to the atrocities of the Catholic
> inquisition to the Italian renaissance assassinators to the ruthless
> Bismarks to the individually depraved Marquis de Sade types.[3]

And, sadly, the list goes on. In the twentieth century we've seen the
effects of the Nazi atrocities and the Holocaust; the fatal failure of
the Vietnam war; the genocide in the ex-Yugoslavia territories; the
genocidal campaigns across the world, including Rwanda, Iraq,
Libya, Syria, and other Middle Eastern territories, and many more
blatant examples of human atrocities. The list of human psychosis
is too long to recount, too incomprehensible to understand, and too

horrific to want to remember. It is a long history of trauma, adding to the collective psychotic pathogen of the Wounded Mind. Political theorist Hannah Arendt famously coined the term the 'banality of evil' to refer to the almost meaningless or indifferent attitude to such afflictions of horror.

Forbes comes from the perspective of the indigenous Native Americans and from the history of his ancestors he has accumulated not only a wealth of experiential information but also a distanced perspective upon the structure of so-called 'civilized societies'. He comes to the conclusion that a developed society takes the *wetiko* desire for power and channels it into creating highly-disciplined and rigid structures that over the years have managed to conceal their controlling mechanisms through institutionalized conditioning. These institutions then go on to create an established 'pecking order', or hierarchical status, between people. This social status ranking system continues to exploit the general population through more socially 'normalized' means. And as I shall explain in a later chapter, these 'normalized' social status structures are inculcated at a very early age, usually beginning at school.

Of course, once the 'infection' has been placed into peoples' minds, then they begin to spread it themselves. Forbes notes how 'Wetiko people' are always trying to co-opt others into their way of thinking and behaviour. This is because often their own success depends on having other people do their 'dirty work' for them. They thus attempt to convince others through persuasive notions of loyalty and obedience. Ideologies and notions of cultural and racial superiority are also adopted into systems of socialization in order to normalize the *wetikos'* behaviour. Innocent or non-conscious *wetikos* can also be co-opted into this system of behaviour through allurements such as grants, support, employment, etc., which entice them into the illusion of individual freedom and personal power.

The *wetiko* psychosis is like an ugly infection which seeps into the human mind and tries to grow there. Like any other pathogen it then tries to infect and feed upon others by reinforcing its own corruption of the human mind. The predatory nature of *wetiko*,

Forbes reminds us, can lurk under almost any guise, and is most prevalent in such slogans as 'patriotism', 'profit-seeking', and 'protecting our way of life'. We could say that we have seen recent examples in 'you're either with us or against us.' The *wetiko* mindset (or 'mind virus') assimilates itself through intensive propaganda programmes designed to perpetuate its own self-serving values. In the end, many of our national cultures have become pervaded by myths, narratives, and entrained thinking patterns that perpetuate a *wetiko* society. Our social-cultural collective minds have been invaded by a psychosis that preserves and protects itself within our patterns of conditioning. Yet what if such a mindset is not only preserved within particular cultures but is available to be assimilated through a species collective mindset? This is the question posed by the psychoanalyst and psychologist Carl Gustav Jung.

Jung's Collective Unconscious

Jung was perhaps the first psychologist to fully realize that what we see playing out upon the global stage is largely a projection, or symptom, of the unconscious psyche of humanity. Jung coined the term 'collective unconscious' in his 1916 essay 'The Structure of the Unconscious' and went on to articulate his ideas further in later publications. In his essay 'The Significance of Constitution and Heredity in Psychology' (November 1929) he wrote that 'primordial images' – or 'archetypes' as he came to call them – belonged to an underlying unconscious psyche and were not individually acquired. He stated that the 'psychic stratum', which he called the collective unconscious, was deeply influenced by 'inherited presuppositions'. In this essay Jung wrote that,

> the collective unconscious comprises in itself the psychic life of our ancestors right back to the earliest beginnings. It is the matrix of all conscious psychic occurrences, and hence it exerts an influence that compromises the freedom of consciousness in the highest degree, since it is continually striving to lead all conscious processes back into the old paths.[4]

Importantly, Jung considered that this collective unconscious does not develop individually but is inherited. That is, we inherit a 'psychic life' that is filled with 'occurrences' that stretch back to earliest beginnings. What if a psychosis, such as the *wetiko* pathogen mentioned by Forbes, has already invaded this psychic realm and now manifests as a disturbance in the field of humanity's collective unconscious? We could very well be dealing with a psycho-pathogen – that is, a mind virus – that infects our individual minds from the underlying collective realm.

This is not the realm of fantasy but of very real possibility. Counsellor and dream-therapist Paul Levy, who considers himself a 'wounded healer', also speaks of the *wetiko* psychosis in Jungian terms. He recognizes that if we take the modern analogy of computing, then it is similar to how a virus would enter our computers and install malware or change the coding. Such a mental pathogen would act in the same way by installing its own malware programme in our minds. For most of the time we are unaware of it, as it acts alongside our own 'normal' mind, until a time when it takes over almost completely. Over time our own mental make-up – our psychological state – would adapt the foreign 'invader' and assimilate it into its own functioning as a way of normalization. In other words, we would eventually come to consider it as *our* mind.

This collective psychosis functions as a field phenomenon, and as such it underlies the entire collective field of nonlocal consciousness. The danger here is that each person can potentially be infected by the psychosis simply by not being mindful of their thoughts. Before we know it, we are having malicious or angry *wetiko*-like thoughts, which then could easily manifest into actual behaviour. Who at one time or another hasn't had a mean or nasty thought? The question is – Did this thought originate within us, or did it enter from without? Since the mind virus pathogen – which I refer to as the Wounded Mind – is a nonlocal phenomenon, then it is possible that we all are infected with it to varying degrees. Or, it may be more accurate to say that this mind *has us*. And the worst of it is that most people will be unconscious and unwitting carriers of this pathogen. As Jung said, 'the world powers that rule over humanity, for good or ill, are unconscious psychic factors... We are steeped in a world that was created by our own psyche.'[5]

The writer William Burroughs is famous for believing that he was possessed by an 'ugly spirit' that continued to haunt and plague him throughout life. He once said that, 'Every man has inside himself a parasitic being who is acting not at all to his advantage.'[6] Later in his life Jung was more direct and forthcoming about the dangers lurking within the human psyche. He stated that, 'Indeed, it is becoming even more obvious that it is not famine, not earthquakes, not cancer but man himself who is man's greatest danger to man, for the simple reason that there is no adequate protection against psychic epidemics, which are infinitely more devastating than the worst of natural catastrophes.'[7] Jung was clear that psychic epidemics were a reality and suggested that we are in great danger because the human psyche is in great danger. He once asked – What if something goes wrong with the psyche?

In one sense, this may be interpreted as part of our 'fallen state' in that from the very beginnings humanity unknowingly inherited an 'alien intruder' from within the collective mind. And yet it was only since the early part of the twentieth century that we started to discover – or uncover – the existence of the collective unconscious. And also, thanks in part to the quantum sciences of the twentieth century, we are learning of the quantum field that interconnects all aspects of our known reality. For the majority of human history, it is likely we were the unwitting carriers of an unknown presence within us. As Jung put it:

> Thus the rabble of spooks that were formerly outside have now transported themselves into the psyche of man ... after it became impossible for the demons to inhabit the rocks, woods, mountains, and rivers, they used human beings as much more dangerous dwelling places.[8]

And from the dwelling place of their unwitting hosts, this 'demonic mind' has wreaked havoc upon the world through influencing the mindset, and thus behaviour, of those individuals who have shaped human history. As a final word from Jung on this matter:

Wars, dynasties, social upheavals, conquests, and religions are but the superficial symptoms of a secret psychic attitude unknown even to the individual himself, and transmitted by no historian ... and the whole future, the whole history of the world, ultimately spring as a gigantic summation from these hidden sources in individuals.[9]

These 'hidden sources' may well have been unknown to the majority of humankind yet apparently they were well known to various shamans and sorcerers. And they were spoken of quite frequently by the nagual don Juan in the dealings with his apprentice Carlos Castaneda.

The Predators of the Shaman

There are wide-ranging accounts throughout shamanic and anthropological literature about the otherworldly travels of sages and sorcerers who engage in healing rituals as well as psychic defense. From their perspective, we are vulnerable to psychic invasion and predatory 'energy forces'. Yet in recent times, and more importantly in well-known and popular publishing, perhaps no-one has been as openly explicit as those teachings given by don Juan through the books of Carlos Castaneda. For many readers, these books will be familiar; if not by actual reading experience then at least in name. In my view, the words and 'teachings' given by don Juan are important in our examination of the Wounded Mind, as they are given in a language and context that are understandable to a modern person. They appear not as the 'ramblings of a sorcerer' but rather as words to wake us up.

It will be useful to quote extensively from the books of Carlos Castaneda to make the point. Another feature of Castaneda's books about don Juan is that they show a progression of understanding and penetration into the shaman's world – or, as don Juan called it, the *Way of the Warrior*. That is, when a reader begins with the first book in the series – *Teachings of Don Juan* – they may be forgiven for thinking that this is a pseudo-anthropological adventure into the psychedelic peyote-eating practices of Mexican shamans. As Castaneda's apprenticeship furthers, both he and the reader are taken deeper into the otherworldly realms of energetic realities beyond our own fragile borders. Later in the series of books, when Castaneda is more experienced and matured into the shamanic path, don Juan reveals some 'truths' to him regarding the nature of the predators. And this is where it gets both interesting and relevant for us.

The narrative on the existence of the 'predators' begins when don Juan, in an almost casual tone, says that − 'There are scores of outside forces controlling you at this moment... The control that I am referring to is something outside the domain of language. It is your control and at the same time it is not. It cannot be classified, but it can certainly be experienced. And above all, it can certainly be manipulated.'[10] When Castaneda questions what these types of 'outside forces' are that impose control upon us, don Juan explains that the ancient sorcerer-shamans discovered that humans have a companion for life. He goes on to say that: 'We have a predator that came from the depths of the cosmos and took over the rule of our lives. Human beings are its prisoners. The predator is our lord and master. It has rendered us docile, helpless. If we want to protest, it suppresses our protest. If we want to act independently, it demands that we don't do so.'[11] Castaneda immediately rejects this statement as he cannot logically process it. It sounds too fantastical. Don Juan, with a characteristic grin, continues:

> Think for a moment, and tell me how you would explain the contradiction between the intelligence of man the engineer and the stupidity of his systems of beliefs, or the stupidity of his contradictory behaviour... They are the ones who set up our hopes and expectations and dreams of success or failure. They have given us covetousness, greed, and cowardice. It is the predators who make us complacent, routinary, and egomaniacal.[12]

Naturally, Castaneda is still unconvinced. 'But how can they do this, don Juan?' he asks. At this point he senses an energy of anger swell up within him. 'Do they whisper all that in our ears while we are asleep?' Here, Castaneda is torn between incredulity and a rising sense of being violated. It is as this point that don Juan lands the stinging blow:

'No, they don't do it that way. That's idiotic!' don Juan said, smiling. 'They are infinitely more efficient and organized than that. In order to keep us obedient, meek and weak, the predators engaged themselves in a stupendous maneuver – stupendous, of course, from the point of view of a fighting strategist. A horrendous maneuver from the point of view of those who suffer it. They gave us their mind! Do you hear me? The predators give us their mind which becomes our mind. The predators' mind is baroque, contradictory, morose, and filled with the fear of being discovered any minute now ... Through the mind, which after all, is their mind, the predators inject into the lives of human beings whatever is convenient for them. And they ensure, in this manner, a degree of security to act as a buffer against their fear.'[13]

And here we have the critical correspondence with the Wounded Mind. According to don Juan, an 'alien' presence, or energy, has infiltrated the human mind. That is, when 'we' are thinking, or 'having' thoughts, we are in effect manifesting – or being influenced by – a corrupted mind that is 'baroque, contradictory, morose' and filled with fear. Is this at all possible? When we connect and engage with the collective unconscious, or the collective mindset, are we in fact tapping into a psyche that, in the words of Jung, stretches 'right back to the earliest beginnings'? Yet those beginnings may also include the 'alien mind' of the predator.

In considering this, Castaneda admits that, 'Whatever don Juan was proposing was preposterous, incredible. At the same time, it was a most reasonable thing, so simple. It explained every kind of human contradiction I could think of. But how could one have taken all this seriously?'[14] Castaneda reflects on a question that is sure to be within us all – how can we take such an idea seriously? Already our minds will be fighting this possibility, or complacently shrugging it off as fictional ramblings suited to psychedelic minds. But what if this response is itself a programmed survival mechanism from the predatory mind? In this encounter, Castaneda also realized how quickly his mind fought against these ideas. He says that, 'I noticed, however, how quickly I rallied my energy to deny everything he had said. After an instant of panic, I began to laugh, as if don Juan had told me a joke.'[15] This response-mechanism was first to deny it and then to make a joke of it – much like we do against many ideas in our own lives!

And yet there was also a niggling sensation that something was beginning to make sense, no matter the apparent strangeness of it. Castaneda continues by saying that,

> No matter how hard I tried, I couldn't discard his logic. The more I thought about it, and the more I talked to and observed myself and my fellow men, the more intense the conviction that something was rendering us incapable of any activity or any interaction or any thought that didn't have the self as its focal point... The unavoidable question that I posed to myself was: Is he influencing me to see this, or is there really a foreign mind dictating everything we do? I lapsed, perforce, into denial again, and I went insanely from denial to acceptance to denial.[16]

Don Juan refers to the predator invasion as the *flyers' mind* and their presence as the *foreign installation*. He suggests that without it most of us would be lost, and that its trickery makes sure it has no competitors to challenge it – ' "You see, the *flyers' mind* has no competitors", don Juan continued. "When it proposes something, it agrees with its own proposition, and it makes you believe that you've done something of worth." '[17] This sleight-of-hand trick, similar to the Magician's Tale in Chapter One, manipulates our mind to find agreement with its own internal narrative, whatever its source may be.

Following this uncomfortable logic, we would suppose that the majority of people are carriers for this predatory – or wounded – mind. And this is where don Juan lands his second blow:

> 'The weird idea,' he said slowly, measuring the effect of his words, 'is that every human being on this earth seems to have exactly the same reactions, the same thoughts, the same feelings. They seem to respond in more or less the same way to the same stimuli. Those reactions seem to be sort of fogged up by the language they speak, but if we scrape that off, they are exactly the same reactions that besiege every human being on Earth.'[18]

As a species, humanity accesses a collective unconscious mind that forms the basis of our thinking patterns and our behavioural traits.

If an element of psychosis, trauma, dominant narrative – i.e., *wetiko* – has infiltrated this collective mental field, then it is a very real possibility that we too have inherited what I call the Wounded Mind. And it is this possibility that is likely to be the source of our inhumane and inconsistent behaviour on this planet as a so-called sentient species. Quite literally, we have a malware in our collective programme – and it's *messing with our minds.*

As an interesting side note, English writer Colin Wilson published a science-fiction-horror novel in 1967 called *The Mind Parasites.* In this book the main protagonist – a Professor Gilbert Austin – makes the remarkable discovery that the human race is being 'attacked by a sort of mind cancer'. After a process of self-examination, he comes to the realization that a form of mind parasite is lurking deep within the layers of the human unconscious. These malignant beings have controlled the inner space of humanity in order to block any discovery, or to thwart the attempts by anyone who suspects their existence. From their dwelling place of the human unconscious, they are able to maintain their parasitic control over the dominant species upon the earth.[*] This storyline is remarkably prescient to our subject here. It also raises the question of what type of civilization or society would such a parasite-predator-psychosis-pathogen wish to create?

The answer to this may lie with a form of twentieth-century theosophy that was put forward by the Austrian-philosopher and mystic Rudolf Steiner.

The Coming of Ahriman

In transcripts of Rudolf Steiner's lectures from the early part of the twentieth-century, he makes mention of an entity he calls Ahriman. For Steiner, this Ahriman is a supersensible being that wishes to distract humanity from aligning with its evolutionary potential and developmental source (i.e., a divine source). In order to accomplish this, it seeks to influence the minds of humanity to develop along a

---

[*] See *The Mind Parasites* by Colin Wilson (recently republished in 2015).

specific path; one that aligns with Ahriman's own needs rather than that of humanity's. Although Steiner only spoke on the subject of Ahriman on few occasions, he was specific about what type of society/civilization was its goal.

The conditions that the ahrimanic presence wishes to create includes the following: a materialistic, mechanical conception of the universe; a rational-materialistic based scientific dogma; an economic view of social dynamics and systems; a strong feature of nationalism and national identities; the popularity of separatist party politics; the prevalence of fundamentalism in religious dogma; and the dominance of an arid, dry intellectual culture.

Well, I would say that this just about sums up the current state of the Western world! It would appear that this ahrimanic presence has been quite successful so far. Steiner was also explicit in stating that the most dangerous aspect of Ahriman would be for this presence to go unrecognized, for it seeks to be hidden (similar to the predators). Steiner, in one of his lectures, said that – '... think of everything that presses us down upon the earth, that makes us dull and philistine, leading us to develop materialistic attitudes, penetrating us with a dry intellect, and so on: there you have a picture of ahrimanic powers.'[19]

The ahrimanic powers, we are told, have a firm intention to get the human domain, as well as the earth, into their sphere of power, and to make human beings dependent upon their control. Again, it sounds eerily familiar. Steiner tells us that Ahriman intends to conceal from us that modern intellectual, rationalistic science is in fact a great illusion, a deception. The idea, apparently, is to keep us all so dulled with our materialistic paradigms that we have no inclination or urge to go seeking for knowledge concerning 'soul and spirit in the cosmos'. Steiner tells us that,

> The intellectualism prevailing among people today is not capable of demonstrating the *inner* potentialities and values of anything... People today prefer to let their intellect remain on the surface and not to penetrate with deeper forces to those levels where the essential nature of things is disclosed.[20]

As I shall discuss later, we are experiencing the 'modern malaise' of a materialistic paradigm that was recently fostered through ideals of modernity, in the West specifically. This materialism – which we can also called 'hyper-modernity' – seems to be almost exactly what Steiner is describing here.

In his lectures Steiner continued to describe the means whereby the ahrimanic impulse would seek to control the minds of humanity. He explained that this being/presence would manipulate our emotions in order to fragment and divide us into small groups (the age-old 'divide and rule' policy). These separate groups would then be encouraged, or manipulated, into attacking one another. Steiner warns us that the ahrimanic powers are working wherever disharmonies arise between groups of people. In one of his lectures Steiner stated that,

> Whatever can separate people into groups, whatever can alienate them from mutual understanding the whole world over and drive wedges between them, strengthens Ahriman's impulse... One group will prove one thing, another its exact opposite, and as both proofs can be shown to be equally logical, hatred and bitterness – of which there is more than enough in the world – will be intensified.[21]

The Ahrimanic powers use everything at their disposal to seed discontent, disarray, and conflict. They manipulate notions of heredity – family, race, tribe, peoples – to create confusion and division. Through these class structures they enforce the dominant cultural paradigm of economic and material needs.

Steiner warns his listeners that the 'ahrimanic incarnation' will be greatly advanced if people fail to develop an independent life of the spirit. It is imperative that we do not allow ourselves to be dragged into the deliberate entanglements of a material, economic, political life. We must be alert, Steiner warns us, to serve our own higher, spiritual development. To fail to do so will only support and further maintain the ahrimanic presence within our lives. In prescient words, Steiner told that – 'You must realize that there is no better way to prepare for Ahriman's cunning efforts to capture the whole earth for his own purposes than that human beings should continue to live an abstract life, steeping themselves in abstractions, as they do in contemporary society.'[22] We have been warned.

In all the examples and cultural contexts described in this chapter — indigenous Native American, Western psychology, Central American shamanism, and European theosophy — we have come to a more expanded and nuanced understanding of the proposition of what I term the *Wounded Mind*. The source of this trauma is still unclear and up for debate. It may be either a collective psychosis of civilization, a predatory invasion, a devolutionary impulse/presence, or a combination of these. Or else it may be something other but with similar aspects. Yet whatever may be the root cause, it is still clear that a traumatic presence lingers within the collective psyche of humanity, and it needs to be recognized for what it is — and expelled. Perhaps the traumas we are seeing inflicted upon the world today are part of this expulsion — a sort of public exorcism. In any case, we need to curtail these 'foreign impulses' in order to evolve toward our destiny as a human species upon this planet.

I now propose we take a further look into the features and characteristics of what I call the Wounded Mind.

Chapter Three

The Wounded Mind

I pushed my soul in a deep dark hole and then I followed it in
I watched myself crawling out as I was a-crawling in
I got up so tight I couldn't unwind
I saw so much I broke my mind
I just dropped in to see what condition my condition was in

'Just Dropped In (To See What Condition My Condition Was In)'
Kenny Rogers and the First Edition (written by Mickey Newbury)

Life in modern times does not truly reflect the greatness of the human spirit. I have suggested that there is the possibility for the existence of some kind of infection/invasion/contagion that produces a form of mental 'madness' that is so normalized within us that we hardly recognize its presence. That is, this 'presence' has embedded itself into our various forms of social conditioning (or perhaps even produces this conditioning) in order to veil its existence. This *normalized madness* then usurps genuine thinking patterns, with the result that when everyone shares the collective psychosis then the madness of the world appears to be a 'normal feature' of human civilization. And those people who are 'awake' to the genuine human spirit and mind are considered the crazies – the anomalies – as the following tale shows:

There was once a wise and powerful king who ruled in a remote city of a far kingdom. And the king was feared for both his might and his love of wisdom. At the heart of the city was a well whose water was cool and crystalline, and all the inhabitants drank from this well, even the king and his courtiers, because there was no other well in the city. One night, while everyone was asleep, a witch entered the city and poured seven drops of a strange liquid into the well, and said:

'From now on, anyone who drinks this water will go crazy.'

The next morning all the inhabitants drank the water from the well, except the king and his lord chamberlain, and very soon everyone went mad, as the witch had foretold. During that day, all people went through the narrow streets and public places whispering to each other:

'The king is mad. Our king and his lord chamberlain have lost their reason. Naturally, we cannot be ruled by a mad king. We must dethrone him!'

That night, the king ordered a golden cup of water from the well to be brought to him. And when they brought the cup the king and his lord chamberlain drank heavily from it. Soon after that there was great rejoicing in that distant city of a far kingdom because the king and his lord chamberlain had regained their reason.

The King and his love of wisdom (Genuine Mind) was corrupted by the poisonous drops of the witch's liquid (virus/pathogen) that resulted in the mass epidemic of craziness (*wetiko*/psychosis/ Wounded Mind). This corrupted mind then became the dominant narrative that influenced social behaviour. This Wounded Mind is like a contagion that infects.

Our collective 'cultural mind' is continually being shaped by dominant social-cultural narratives that normalize our mental and emotional behavioural patterns. These norms are then transferred into cultural myths that serve to transmit and reinforce these belief systems in the minds of the masses. We end up validating our own corrupted thinking through unconscious affirmations. Once this seed of psychosis is planted, then it aims to propagate and strengthen through diversions and manifestations that legitimate its own 'logical' existence. It is likely to want to drown out our authentic inner voice as a number one priority. Like a mental cancer, it ingratiates itself into our own neural pathways as an insider rather than an *outsider* so that we fail to notice its toxic presence. It then continues to invest heavily in its own way of thinking so as to erase any doubt within the person/carrier's mind (similar to don Juan's descriptions). Yet there certainly must be a niggling sense of something being 'not-quite-right' deep within any sensible/sensitive person.

Whether rationally, instinctively, or deep in our hearts, most of us know that something is not right about human culture and social behaviour. Human life is not yet in balance. It is as if we continue to live under the conditioning of the contagious 'old mind' of humanity; one that operates through control, conflict, censorship, and consumerism. In this way our contemporary societies are increasingly centred around emotion to a degree that allows people to be distracted, at the same time as being entertained like never before. This strange reality of ours becomes internalized so that we adapt to a form of 'normality', and anyone who speaks up or questions this 'paradigm of normality' is considered either odd, eccentric or, at worst, crazy. A more recent category for such people is now to be designated as a 'conspiracy theorist', which is a quick way to dismiss people with ideas or thinking contrary to this 'norm'. And those people who appear to accept and encourage such norms are quickly brought 'into the fold' and supported in their career paths. Our social structures praise and put up as role models those figures who embody these materialistic-economic ideals, especially noticeable within capitalist industry and politics, where power and control are dominant yet lauded values.

The majority of those manifesting the Wounded Mind are not in psychiatric care but running most of our social, political, and financial institutions. Positions of great power necessitate their own specific mindset, one that is generally provided by the corrupted mind.

A Disturbance of Mind

The presence of the Wounded Mind is like a sickness of the soul, and it manifests as a disturbance in the collective unconscious. Just like any other virus or pathogen, it seeks to spread itself by infecting as many carriers as possible. Those people who carry the Wounded Mind (whether knowingly or not) act as transmitters and amplifiers for it, strengthening its frequency within the collective nonlocal field of consciousness. As Paul Levy notes, 'People who are channeling the vibratory frequency of wetiko align with each other through psychic resonance to reinforce their unspoken shared agreement so as to uphold their deranged view of reality.'[1] A collective possession is what we refer to as a psychic epidemic, or a disturbance in the field. Such disturbances can have varying affects upon people's mental health and well-being.

People who suffer from a Wounded Mind may carry it as an 'undefinable' trauma within them, and it is common to turn to alcoholism or drug dependencies as a way of coping (or of escape). When a person feels stressed or traumatized, they are like an open wound for further mental invasion. And it can be quite subtle at first as our modern societies have devised endless ways for intervening in our lives. We are distracted to look away from our own minds and thus miss the psycho-pathogen in action. As a person further integrates the Wounded Mind they may find themselves vulnerable to victimization; such as through social harassment and bullying (especially online nowadays), or as addicted-consumers of sexual deviancy, pornography, and socially-sanctioned extreme experiences. The monk Thomas Merton said that our modern societies suffer from a crisis of sanity:

> The problems of the nations are the problems of mentally deranged people, but magnified a thousand times because they have the full-straight-faced approbation of a schizoid society, schizoid national structures, schizoid military and business complexes.[2]

If all modern institutions are infected by a corrupted system of mental thinking patterns, then as Merton suggests, this instability will be amplified and made worse. Individual neuroses are given institutional sanction and support within a culture that has based its social norms upon such irrationalities. The irrational has broken through and implanted itself as the rational standard rule. It is perhaps little wonder that people can be so susceptible to this mental pathogen when it comes to us dressed up in sheep's clothing. As is always the case, those people most vulnerable are usually those who are conditioned to authority and or passivity. This trait is one that is first implanted through compulsory schooling (see Chapter 4).

Likewise, people who are easily influenced by external opinions, and whom are prone to group-thinking, are amongst the first to give away their mental independence to external sources. The virus of the Wounded Mind preys upon such 'group-think' individuals as they are the mass open playing-fields for psychic epidemics. As Jack Forbes notes, many people are not independent selves: 'Many are puppets or pimps, whose strings are pulled by others or who follow a life-path dictated by others. Thus they are ripe for the *wetiko* infection.'[3] The 'mass mind' of humanity helps in the transmission and proliferation of the *wetiko* virus. Conscious awareness is our greatest antidote. As the psychiatrist R.D. Laing once said — 'The condition of alienation, of being asleep, of being unconscious, of being out of one's mind, is the condition of the normal man ... normal men have killed perhaps 100,000,000 of their fellow normal men in the last fifty years.'[4]

If we are to see human history from a wider perspective, then it is important we view major events, human actions, propaganda, social disturbances, power struggles, and the rest, from this standpoint of the *wetiko* virus. As Jack Forbes explains in his book *Columbus and other Cannibals*, the *wetiko* personality is formed from many traits that include greed, lust, ambition, materialism, insincerity, and a 'split' personality. In all, these are traits that mark a lack of authenticity. The Wounded Mind — a.k.a. *wetiko* virus — seeks to develop greater degrees of inauthenticity and lack of empathy within the individual. These people, he says, are the 'pimps' who follow other people's orders, and refuse to take responsibility for their own actions. Such a person, he says, cannot be authentic:

> Such a person is not merely a pimp, he is also a ghost, as it were, a mere imitation of a person. His life is an imitation of life, lacking solidity and realness. But the *wetiko* world is full of such pimps and ghosts.[5]

The question then is how to resist the spread of the pathogen?

The peril of the Wounded Mind is that resistance may also help to spread it. That is, people who often start out resisting and fighting against this corrupted mindset often find themselves adopting its values in order to survive. It's the 'if you can't beat them, join them' type of thinking. And this cliché too is very likely to have been a product of the Wounded Mind intending to verify itself (as don Juan said). It may seem that we are struggling to awaken against our very own spell of sleep.

Under the Pathogen Spell

It has often been said – by mystics, sages, and wisdom traditions – that humanity is collectively asleep. As a species we move through our lives, active within a waking dream state: our ignorance over our condition, and the absence of real knowledge, indicates we are asleep. Similarly, the Gnostics viewed humanity as being 'asleep' under a trance – a form of material spell – that has severed us from contact with a genuine divine source. Instead, we are ruled by a false or 'flawed god', a demiurge, that has malevolent intentions to keep us trapped within the material realms.

Modern science informs us constantly that the 'physical' universe is not materially substantial in the way we had thought, or previously were told. It is a dimension of energy that coalesces, or coagulates, into dense arrangements that we experience as matter. Our space-time continuum is not empty but consists of highly-dense energy that forms a non-local field. Modern scientific philosophers also hypothesize that this non-local field is conscious.[*] Everything in our physical universe is a projection, or secondary manifestation, from this underlying non-local field. Similarly, human consciousness exists as a non-local phenomenon, operating both within the human mind-body complex as well as without. This perspective helps us to understand how a mental virus – the *wetiko* pathogen – could infect and affect human life regardless of location and physical proximity. Psychic energy operates within the non-local field and as a species we are connected in what we could term a 'species mind' across the planet, like a mental membrane.

The reality in which we live is suffused with our mental projec-

---

[*] See *What is Reality?* by Ervin Laszlo (Select Books, 2016).

tions. As Jung taught, our unconscious thoughts form a part of the world, just as do our conscious thoughts. We should not view the physical world as being distinct or separate from our mental worlds. This human blind spot – to see our actions and thoughts as separate from the world around us – has been the cause of all our suffering as well as our environmental cruelty. Each person is constantly interacting and communicating with a world of non-visible thought, unknown to the great majority of us. And this is how the mental pathogen is able to operate with virtual impunity. Like an invisible infection, we can be impregnated with a thought-virus that then begins to spread once within our mental faculties. And modern societies have begun to foster this mental pathogen by developing cultural systems and normative thinking patterns that mirror its corrupted form.

The more we breed this Wounded Mind within our societies and cultures, the more people will behave and live like automatons. We will live within a tighter range of conditioned stimuli that pro-grammes specific opinions and thinking patterns that validate the pathogen. As I have said, a person who is more conditioned to obedience is more susceptible to receive the mental *wetiko* virus. Perhaps this is why our modern societies are establishing rigid orders of control and obedience, such as when we travel, pass through airports, etc. It can be likened to a preparation for auto-mated behaviour as a requisite for an automated mind. The mystic George Gurdjieff wrote:

> Contemporary culture requires automatons. And people are undoubtedly losing their acquired habits of independence and turning into automatons, into parts of machines... Man is becoming a willing slave. He no longer needs chains. He begins to grow fond of his slavery, to be proud of it. And this is the most terrible thing that can happen to a man.[6]

By adopting the mentality of the Wounded Mind, we participate in our own suppression and further the behaviour of an auto-maton. We need to recognize that many of our incumbent social systems are set-up to corroborate and reinforce the consensus mind-set. Any genuine resistance cannot come from any 'mass movement' but only from those persons who can think and act independently.

To wake up to the fact of our slumbering participation within the collective psycho-pathogen can be both traumatizing and yet liberating. It is not a pleasant realization to see how we've been inundated with a form of mental madness. We need to recognize that the Wounded Mind is a field phenomenon, and that our own mind and thoughts do not exist securely guarded within our heads. Since we are all interconnected within the non-local field, we are all susceptible to the infection of this predatory virus. The first step we can take is to accept the possibility that the pathogen virus exists. The Gnostic text *The Gospel of Philip* says: 'So long as the root of wickedness is hidden, it is strong. But when it is recognized, it is dissolved. When it is revealed, it perishes...' The danger lies in our distraction.

We must guard against being diverted away from our authenticity and lured into the modern distractions of hedonistic pleasure-seeking, greed and materialism, and the pursuit of shallow satisfactions. In short, we need to guard against being lured away from the genuine call of our own spirit and essence. For this illusive psychosis offers false promises:

> The *wetiko* psychosis is a sickness of the spirit that takes people down an ugly path with no heart. They may kill, but they are not warriors. They may learn skills, but they acquire no wisdom. They may be surrounded by death but they do not, or cannot, learn its message. They chase after the riches or rewards of a transient world and delude themselves into believing that big tombs and monuments can make it permanent.[7]

Our modern cultures appear to want to prevent the majority of people from pursuing their own spiritual paths. This is no doubt because our capitalist consumer-based societies require a regular mass of workers and consumers who live a regulated, predictable, and conformist life. As discussed in the next chapter, obedience and passivity to the system is the objective of our societal training – and not genuine self-development. We are wounded as we are processed by our social systems and we need to find our healing.

The Wounded Healer

The only true alternative to the Wounded Mind lies in the resilience and resistance of the human spirit. Our wisdom traditions are replete with teachings of how to deal with the psychosis that has entered human life. This mental pathogen, whether it is called the *wetiko* psychosis or the Wounded Mind, is really a sickness or disease of the human spirit. To overcome its influence we need to turn inward to find strength and support. We need to connect with the essence of our humanity and be guided by our intuitions. And this requires both recognition as well as responsibility.

It would be a false gesture to adjust ourselves to such a corrupted system as we would eventually become corrupted ourselves. Yet we would likely not notice this as the insanity of the Wounded Mind would have become the norm. Again, we are reminded of the popular quote cited earlier from Krishnamurti – 'It is *no measure* of health to be well adjusted to a profoundly sick society.'

We can recognize the presence of the Wounded Mind when it enters into our thinking as it seeks to strengthen the rational 'logical' component and attempts to over-intellectualize everything. This 'false psyche' that implants itself into us brings along its own convoluted logic. This topsy-turvy nonsensical thinking is an inversion of true values. It is responsible for developing what I call the 'old mind' thinking patterns; namely the values of conquest, competition, censorship, and control. Such terror as it can produce doesn't need to come from guns or bombs (although this is one unfortunate form); it seeks coercion, compliance, and ultimately control, by manipulation and malicious influence. Such control can come from unknowing school teachers, bullying authority figures, as well as greedy financiers; all of whom place us under influence, force us into passivity, or emasculate us through debt. And such enforcers may wear the smartest or the most expensive of clothes and come with a smile upon their faces.

Yet by fighting the system head-on, especially with similar tools of protest, we continue to feed power into the incumbent structures. As the visionary Buckminster Fuller famously said — 'You never change things by fighting the existing reality. To change something, build a new model that makes the existing model obsolete.'* The parallel mistake would be to struggle with our own mind and to further develop the dualisms within ourselves.† Physicist and thinker David Bohm was also aware of this mental infection and considered, especially in his later life, how we might combat this problem:

> It's similar to a virus — somehow this is a disease of thought, of knowledge, of information, spreading all over the world. The more computers, radio, and television we have, the faster it spreads. So the kind of thought that's going on all around us begins to take over in every one of us, without our even noticing it. It's spreading like a virus and each one of us is nourishing that virus ... The only way to stop it is to recognize it, to acknowledge it, to see what it is. If any one of us starts to look at that, then we are looking at the source of the problem.[8]

Precisely. It is necessary to see something for what it is — recognition and acknowledgement is key. Otherwise we are vulnerable to not only unseen manipulations but also the subtle yet powerful energies of discouragement. Here is a tale about the price of discouragement:

> Once the word spread that the devil was pulling out of his business and was arranging to sell-off all his tools of the trade to the highest bidder. The night of the sale all the tools were arranged for the bidders to view. What a motley crew it was! There were sinister tools of hatred, jealousy, envy, malice, treachery, plus all the other elements of evil. Yet besides these there was also an instrument that seemed harmless, a wedge-shaped instrument that appeared worn out, shabby, and yet was priced so much higher than all others. Someone asked the devil what the name of such a poor-looking instrument was.

---

* A popular phrase that can be found easily in the public domain.

† See my earlier book *The Struggle for your Mind* (2012).

'Discouragement', answered the Devil.

'And why is the price so high for such a non-malicious sounding instrument? asked the bidder.

'Because', spoke the Devil, 'this instrument is more useful to me than any other. I can enter the consciousness of a human being when all other ways fail me and once inside through the discouragement of that person, I can do whatever I please. The instrument is worn out because I use it almost everywhere and as very few people know about this I can continue to successfully achieve my goals.'

And as the price of discouragement was so very, very high even today it remains a tool in the property of the Devil.

The price of discouragement is a high price too many of us continue to pay. Through this, and other ways, we are a multitude of wounded persons in need of healing.

The archetype of the 'wounded healer', coined by Jung, refers to those people (generally psychologists, therapists, etc.) who feel compelled to treat others because of having been 'wounded', or having experienced some form of trauma themselves. A personal experience of trauma may serve as a catalytic process that can later help to facilitate healing within others. Since as a species we share a collective psyche (the collective unconscious, as Jung would say), then we also share in the collective wound of humanity. Each of us can be both a recipient of the Wounded Mind as well as a potential healer for ourselves and others.

Our very real struggles today are not the distractions that are pushed onto us through our mainstream media – the political farce, national rivalries, shallow ideologies, opinions, and fear-mongering – but between the inner freedom of the human spirit and the constraints of our mentally-corrupted societies and cultures. We need to ask ourselves the question that don Juan posed to his student Carlos Castaneda – 'Then ask yourself, and yourself alone, one question... Does this path have a heart? If it does, the path is good, if it doesn't it is of no use.'[9] The most important things in the world are not to be found in any place external to us. I have a wooden-painted plaque given to me by a dear friend that hangs in this room as I write. Upon it is written

— 'Motto of This House: the most important things in life are not THINGS.'

Any society or culture that does not recognize and support the human as a spiritual being will ultimately be lacking in a viable, long-term future. The dominant thinking patterns of the world today promote and encourage us to live out our lives within a material framework, giving in to our lower nature and passions, forever dependent upon materialistic needs and desires. Meaning is an abstract thing, provided for by working lives given to the system that educates and trains us not to think against it. We are made to feel content by basic and often crude satisfactions rather than being encouraged to develop our finer intuitions and percipient human spirit. We are discouraged, or even blocked, from acting or thinking creatively against the incumbent system.

If we cannot bring harmony and good sense to the world around us, then we should at least bring it upon ourselves. We are the wounded ones who can become our own wounded healers. Until we do so, we exist as ghosts in the modern machine.

Chapter Four

Ghosts in the Modern Machine

'The function of these collective rituals we call school has very little to do with intellectual development... The collective rituals of lower grades are about habit training, about practicing attention and fealty to authority. In this way, independent consciousness can be undermined in its formative stages.'

John Taylor Gatto, *Weapons of Mass Instruction*

'People say that what we are all seeking is the meaning for life. I don't think that's what we're really seeking. I think what we're seeking is an experience of being alive.'

Joseph Campbell

Until we can recognize that many of us have imbibed the Wounded Mind then we continue to go about our lives like ghosts in the machine, repeating the mantra of the conditioning implanted in us from an early age. And the wounding begins from the early years of our childhood through compulsory schooling. The programming must reach us early before we can become fully-formed adults. It is like trying to learn a new language when in middle age. It is very difficult for the majority of us because our minds and linguistic pathways are already programmed, and we need to create space for a new set of linguistic learning to enter. Yet in childhood our minds are ripe for the picking. Is it any wonder that we have seen a rise of student violence, learning deficiencies or increase in medication usage within the educational institutions? These are our formative years where the hearts and minds of young souls are nurtured and developed. Or rather, that is the illusion or fantasy, as I will explain.

Historian Yuval Noah Harari notes how in 2011, 3.5 million American children were taking medications for ADHD (attention deficit hyperactivity disorder). In the UK the number rose from 92,000 in 1997 to 786,000 in 2012.[1] That's a huge increase by anyone's standards, and there should be no excuse for it. The majority of drug prescriptions for children were for the drug methylphenidate, better known by one of its brand names, Ritalin. In the US, those children between the ages of six to twelve were taking the most prescription drugs. Similarly, in Australia, the use of stimulant drugs to treat ADHD in children, such as Ritalin, had risen intensely by up to 300% between 2002 and 2009.[2] This may be not so much a medical condition but rather a clinical trend to treat more-or-less 'once normal' behaviour with a pharmacological response. I expect the numbers have been rising each year as the situation becomes worse rather than better. It is no good to solve the situation by throwing medication, stricter rules, armed guards, or now even weaponry at it. The incidence of gun-related violence and killings in US schools is absurd. There are almost annual massacres where innocent people (students and teachers) are assassinated by someone with a grudge – and a gun. Just recently there was a shooting massacre at the Marjory Stoneman Douglas High School in Florida where on 14 February 2018, a 19-year-old former student gunned down scores of people. Seventeen people were murdered and sixteen others were wounded. It was certainly not the first of its kind, and sadly, nor will it be the last. What has happened to transform places of study and learning into pharma-fuelled laboratories of conditioning, boredom, and rage?

In the far past, students were apprentices that learnt a skill. They studied and either learnt great skills or they didn't. They were tested by a live ability of their skill, not by numbers. The industrial age brought the marks system into a mass programme of compulsory schooling. Students now get 80 or 75 or 60. Our institutions and modern societies measure the worth of an individual according to these grades, which then follow them around for the rest of their lives as a 'status mark'. It is no coincidence that the rise of industrial nations saw the rise of compulsory schooling, as it served to create a nation of potential workers. When automated workers are required as cogs in the machine, then the last thing the system wants are creative, visionary individuals with minds of their own. The collective mind had to be corrupted into conformity. Schooling became the hidden hand for the Wounded Mind to infect with impunity.

The Artificial Extension of Childhood

Lifelong schoolteacher and educator John Taylor Gatto refers to compulsory schooling as the 'artificial extension of childhood'. That is, many of our schools, in the 'modern' world especially, have become factories of childishness, where children are forced to grow older without growing up. Most of us see no problems with school; after all, did we not go through the same experience ourselves? Are we not normal, sane, and adjusted citizens of our country (whatever that means)? And is it just a coincidence that the formal categorization of 'adolescence' arrived around the time when compulsory schooling was being established into organized state bodies and strict governance? It is generally agreed upon by psychologists that the formal study of adolescence began with the publication in 1904 of G. Stanley Hall's influential work *Adolescence: Its Psychology and Its Relations to Physiology, Anthropology, Sociology, Sex, Crime and Religion*. Hall, and subsequently the American Psychological Association, viewed adolescence as a time of internal upheaval. That is, adolescence was institutionally 'identified' as an irrational and uncertain period of growth that required 'psychological controls' during its period. These controls, it was decided, could be provided by rigorous schooling.

It is also worth noting that Hall based his ideas strongly upon Darwin's theory of evolution as well as the theories of Sigmund Freud. Hall was highly anti-individualist and believed that the individual should be subsumed into the collective. As such, he was an ideal channel for the dissemination of the Wounded Mind. Hall argued that child development displays his highly-racialized view of human history from the perspective of Darwinian evolutionary development. In other words, he saw pre-adolescent children as savages and that reasoning with them was a waste of time. Children, he believed, must simply be taught to fear and love through authoritarian discipline, which included the use of corporal punishment. And one more thing; Hall was a proponent of racial eugenics. An almost perfect match, it seems, for the psychological narrative needed to frame the re-organization of industrial-era schooling in the early twentieth century.

Around the same time, the journalist and cultural critic H.L. Mencken wrote that,

> The most erroneous assumption is to the effect that the aim of public education is to fill the young of the species with knowledge and awaken their intelligence, and so make them fit to discharge the duties of citizenship in an enlightened and independent manner. Nothing could be further from the truth. The aim of public education is not to spread enlightenment at all; it is simply to reduce as many individuals as possible to the same safe level, to breed and train a standardized citizenry, to put down dissent and originality. That is its aim in the United States, whatever the pretensions of politicians, pedagogues and other such mountebanks, and that is its aim everywhere else.[3]

Despite the altruistic rhetoric to the contrary, it seems most likely that the rise of organized compulsory schooling in the late modern era (1850–1880) coincided with the needs of burgeoning industrial economies. It is an accepted fact that compulsory schooling of this later modern era was based on the Prussian model. It has been criticized widely as 'an educational system deliberately designed to produce mediocre intellects, to hamstring the inner life, to deny students appreciable leadership skills, and to ensure docile and incomplete citizens – all in order to render the populace "manageable".'[4] Later, in the early years of the twentieth century, schooling underwent a vast bureaucratic reorganization, with centralized school boards and inspectors, with the aim to push out local boards that comprised of parents and community figures. The hand of authority would now reach down from above.

What I am trying to convey here is the sense that a specific collective mindset, which has been described as the *wetiko* virus or the Wounded Mind, found a way into compulsory mainstream educational systems and has become entrenched ever since. It is a mental framework that programmes not only how minds should think but importantly how bodies should behave. At an early age, children are divided by subject, grades and rankings, authoritative expectations, and many other subtle means. When combined together, it creates a system that develops separated, docile, and obedient individuals that are pliant in adhering to the collective-consumer life that awaits them. Put this way, it doesn't sound very pleasant at all. In the interests of the development of complex economic and political nations, it would be efficient to have a regulated 'dumbed down' populace that would conform to authority and accept their lot in life. A mind moulded by standardized tests and programmed by mandatory acquiescence would appear ideal to a ruling elite. Yet let's not take my word for it. We should also listen to what others have had to say on the matter.

An early proponent of the Prussian system of compulsory edu-cation was Alexander Inglis whose book *Principles of Secondary Education* (1918) helped to pave the way for the revolution in US schooling between 1905 and 1930. Inglis breaks down the purpose of modern schooling into six basic functions, which are: i) adaptive; ii) integrative; iii) directive; iv) differing; v) selective; and vi) pro-paedeutic (instructive). To expand further on this, the adaptive function requires establishing fixed habits of obedience to author-ity, whilst the integrative requires schoolchildren to conform. The directive function is to determine a child's most likely social role, and the differing requires solidifying and enforcing this chosen social role. The selective function is a Darwinian notion that means recognizing the tagging of the 'unfit' and favouring the prospective, whilst finally propaedeutic (or instructive) means grooming a selection of children to become teachers (or caretakers) in order to continue the 'educational' project. Dr Inglis was in charge of the secondary school textbook publishing division at Houghton Mifflin, a primary supplier of school text books. A colleague of Inglis was Ellwood P. Cubberley who was in charge of elementary school texts at Houghton Mifflin. Cubberley had written in his book *Public School Administration* (1922) that 'our schools are ... factories in which the raw products (children) are to be shaped and fashioned... And that it is the business of the school to build its pupils according to the specifications laid down.'[5]

It almost sounds like an intentional conspiracy. Surely, this is not the case. The education of our young children is far too important for anything but their best interests to be at heart. Let us continue our examination. The perspective taken here is largely from a US history of schooling, yet it applies to the general spectrum of modern compulsory schooling. Of course, there are exceptions, noticeably in Finland and similar nations that came later to the industrial juggernaut.

Although these examples so far are largely from the annuals of educational history they show the ideological, and intentional, foundations which spawned their development. And these in-built intentions have not only remained within the system of compulsory schooling but have also strengthened throughout the intervening years. One of these inscribed intentions was stated by William Torrey Harris, US Commissioner of Education from 1889 to 1906, who declared that society needed a tool to develop psychological alienation, so that children would place their dependence upon outside authority. This could best be achieved, he said, within dark, airless corridors. In his *Philosophy of Education* (1906) he wrote that,

> Ninety-nine [students] out of a hundred are automata, careful to walk in prescribed paths, careful to follow the prescribed custom. This is not an accident but the result of substantial education which, sci-entifically defined, is the subsumption of the individual... The great purpose of school can be realized better in dark, airless, ugly places... School should develop the power to withdraw from the external world.[5]

This is a mindset that knows that by developing individual aliena-tion within children, it is easier for them to deal with mundane jobs in a motiveless world, flipping burgers or packing boxes. Such a life can be tolerated better without a rich inner life.

Education was hijacked to become a training ground for implanting a deliberate mindset, one that I have termed the

Wounded Mind. It is this mental virus, or pathogen, that then becomes assimilated into the minds of millions of young school children, creating a large class of automata-workers that subscribe to a consumerist lifestyle. As I have said, it is an inherited collective mind that evades the seeking of an inner life. It is a programming that inculcates the capacity for maintaining the boredom of routine work whilst arresting inner development. Children grow in years yet are kept at a childish, immature stage within. We need to recognize that these goals are not conspiracy-related but are *policy-related*.

Arrested Development

A huge document of government policy named *The Behavioural Science Teacher Education Project* outlined reforms for compulsory schooling to be forcibly implemented on US education after 1967. Its stated aims were to keep track of the common masses and expose it to 'direct or subliminal influence when necessary' in order to develop a society where 'few will be able to maintain control over their own opinions'.[6] The report also told of how 'chemical experimentation' on minors will become normal procedure after 1967 – a foreshadow of today's prescription drug epidemic in classrooms with Ritalin and Adderall use, as mentioned at the beginning of this chapter. And this pathway of arrested development began to have its effects.

One area where this became visible in the United States was in army literacy tests, which were issued as standard as part of soldier recruitment (or conscription). Results showed that army literacy test failures increased greatly throughout the twentieth century. These tests were necessary in order to check that soldiers had the very basic literacy skills for reading instructions. During US conscription for WWII, literacy rates were at 96%. That is, illiteracy was at 4%. By the end of the Vietnam war in 1973, 'the number of men found non-inductible by reason of inability to read safety instructions, interpret road signs, decipher orders – the number found illiterate in other words – had reached 27 percent of the total pool.'[7]

From another perspective, this time academic, the University of Connecticut conducted a study in 2006 to measure how much learning is achieved at university. Five academic areas were selected, using 14,000 students at fifty American colleges, including such prestigious institutions as Yale, Brown, and Georgetown. At sixteen institutions – including Yale, Brown, and Georgetown – graduating seniors knew less than incoming freshmen. This meant that there had been negative growth. Amongst the other 34 institutions, no measurable change had occurred.

It appears that education in our modern societies is serving to de-individualize the students in a system that favours standardization over vision and creativity. No wonder that standardized testing is the bane of student life and the cause of so much stress. In the United States, the Scholastic Assessment Test (known as SAT) states that it measures literacy, numeracy and writing skills needed for 'academic success' in college. And yet the SATS are famous for their use of obscure vocabulary and rigidity. In the spring of 2016 a new revised version of SAT was rolled out that, instead of improving matters, actually reinforced its biases. These tests emphasize speed rather than the ability to show intelligence. They require quick recall and time management over subject knowledge. Again, this emphasizes regurgitation of conditioned learning over individual intelligence. The SATs are designed to rank students – the hierarchical mentality – rather than measuring what the student knows.[*] These ranking labels remain with students throughout their lives and further condition a psychological state of 'status number' or failure – unworthiness. Students have been known to commit suicide or engage in self-harm due to the stress of educational exams, whether in the US (SAT), or in the UK (GCSEs and A levels). Any online search will show a myriad of corroborative evidence for this. Examinations are a 'test-and-punish' form of social ranking that indoctrinates the Wounded Mind into generations of children at a young age.

---

[*] See 'The Big Problem With the New SAT' – https://www.nytimes.com/2015/05/05/opinion/the-big-problem-with-the-new-sat.html

We are led to believe that 'success' correlates with 'schooling' yet this is not true from any intellectual or financial standpoint. This is a myth of our conditioning. In fact, a great number of successful, inventive, and/or rich people have become so through their own self-initiated drives. Do the homework yourselves. Look up the lives of creative and inventive people that have made a mark on the world and see how many of them trace their success to their school training. You might also be surprised how many of these people actually dropped out of school or opted for alternative routes. Compulsory schooling arrests the development of creative, imaginative, and innovative minds. They are a formative training ground preparing a generation of young people for a life where social systems continue to take away our responsibilities, economically (easy credit), culturally (easy social security), emotionally (easy entertainment), and intellectually (easy false answers, or fake news).

In the UK it is reported that: 'Already literacy standards are declining: research has shown that many children are more likely to own a mobile phone than a book.'[8] Sadly, young minds are being colonized and converted into receptacles for the mental pathogen of the Wounded Mind. This prepares them for a future in organized 'modern' society which values people by ranking them into winners and losers, mediocre or elite, credit-borrowers or individuals of 'high-net worth'. Perhaps the only truthful thing about compulsory schooling is that it teaches the young child about their place in the social order, which then lasts a lifetime for most people. We may think we are sending our children to school – to be taught by perfect strangers and to be given information we cannot be sure of – in order to be taught to be smart. But that just isn't the case. We are sending children off to be conditioned into accepting the dominant narrative and to be instructed to conform. Schooling is not based around the interests of the students but exclusively around the wishes of others who act in their own self-interests.

This was cleverly shown by George Orwell in his book *Animal Farm* where a false propaganda that all are equal hides the truth that some are 'more equal than others'. And those dumbed from compulsory schooling are conditioned into being less equal. Look at how schools are increasingly mirroring prisons, especially in the US. Students have to pass through a metal detector before entering school or are searched by armed guards. They cannot go to the toilet without being issued a 'Hall Pass', and their movements are monitored at all times. This type of schooling becomes a laboratory for later society, where monitoring and punishment is trained into them to be always close at hand. From factory schooling to prison – the US now jails 25% of all prisoners on earth. Something is obviously failing people here; or preparing them.

An Absence of Creativity and Context

When a character from Charles Dickens's *Hard Times* asks someone for a definition of a horse, they speak in terms of facts and calculations, showing a manner of literal cognition. They respond with: 'Quadruped. Graminivorous. Forty teeth, namely twenty-four grinders, four eye-teeth, and twelve incisive. Sheds coat in the spring; in marshy countries, sheds hoofs, too. Hoofs hard, but requiring to be shod with iron. Age known by marks in mouth.' Here lie all the facts but none of the context. They have assimilated the dots but are unable to join them, like a memory that cannot synthesize the information and transform it into intelligence. It demonstrates a way of cognition that lacks imagination and integral thought. It is a divisive mind rather than a coherent one. Any genuine learning needs to be about developing imagination and creativity – qualities that develop insight, lateral and quick thinking. Yet no doubt these are also the qualities that are dangerous to the machine-wielding status quo.

Educational neuroscientist John Geake did research on student's brain activities and his 'studies of gifted children revealed that their brains showed greater interconnectivity than the brains of those with average cognitive ability'.[9] That is, they performed the tasks of making connections where they didn't exist before – of connecting the dots, as we say. Real education is about integral perspective, contextual awareness, and making connections. These qualities, when exercised and strengthened, help to develop greater self-awareness. Learning is about coming to know yourself. Otherwise you are another compliant cog within the system of the collective dominant mental paradigm – the Wounded Mind. Self-awareness and self-knowledge is what helps us to integrate with the wider environment, and to live balanced, coherent social lives. The very opposite of this is self-alienation, which if we remember was one of the early declared goals of compulsory schooling – achieved within 'dark, airless, ugly places.'

Throughout the many decades of compulsory schooling within such modern societies as the US and the UK, there has been an erosion of children's imagination and the neglect of their inner life. Classes of art, music, creative writing, and other creative subjects, have been gradually taken off the curriculum. In its place the student is confronted (or traumatized) by endless memory drills and multiple-choice exams, and other forms of standardized testing. The result of this is that, in the US, the National Commission on the Future of Higher Education reported, in August 2006, that, 'Only 31 percent of college-educated Americans can fully comprehend a newspaper story, down from 40 percent a decade ago.'[10] It almost seems as if there is a deliberate policy of keeping people dumb.

John Taylor Gatto taught for thirty years in US public schools and was named New York State's official Teacher of the Year. He resigned the same year and penned the bestseller *Dumbing Us Down: The Hidden Curriculum of Compulsory Schooling*. He notes that whatever education happens in school happens *despite* school and not because of it. Over his many years as a teacher, he came to the tragic realization that learning isn't the actual goal of compulsory schooling. He went on to write, in *Weapons of Mass Instruction*, that:

> The official economy we have constructed demands constantly renewed supplies of leveled, spiritless, passive, anxious, friendless, family-less people who can be scrapped and replaced endlessly, and who will perform at maximum efficiency until their own time comes to be scrap...[11]

If we could all but see through the illusions of mass compulsory schooling, then we would also see through the illusions which hold our modern societies together.

We are being given a collective mind of conformity, where creativity, vision, and the wider integral context is noticeably absent. In its place we have a range of trendy-sounding educational forms such as mastery learning, outcomes-based education, school-to-work, and classroom-business partnerships. They all sound very future-work orientated, yet whose future? And whose work? This is the dominant paradigm at work here, forming a shared mind-like-virus that is spreading through the machine as well as through the machines we use.

Virus in the Machine

We are moving into unknown territory. Young people know this better than most of us. Thinking about the future has perhaps never before presented us with so many contradictory thoughts. We are more certain of our uncertainty than of our future. And yet at the same time our younger generations are being confronted and bombarded with unprecedented impacts, influences, and negative distractions. As I mentioned in Chapter One, a recent study had revealed that in the first twelve years of a child's life, they would have been subjected to around 20,000 murders through television news and programmes, films, online content, and video games.[12] Furthermore, a summary of research finds that:

> The most comprehensive meta-analysis to date has drawn on 136 papers detailing 381 independent tests of association conducted on a total of 130,296 research participants, finding that violent game play led to significant increases in desensitization, physiological arousal, aggressive cognition, and aggressive behaviour, while prosocial behaviour decreased.[13]

This is not a debate on the influences of technology, as that is a complex, two-edged sword. However, it is interesting to note how over recent years technological usage has crept into the lives of young teens and babies to a point of being normalized. A few years ago, the toy giant Fisher-Price released a potty-training seat complete with an i-pad holder for the baby to use whilst learning how to use a toilet. It appears that navigating a touch-screen is something we now learn before we know how correctly to poo. Although pressure emerged to withdraw the product, other companies soon followed to offer a similar i-pad potty. Go and search for it yourself – the i-pad potty is still there.

The same mentality is now function-creeping into compulsory schooling. As an example, a head teacher of a school in Essex in the UK spoke about how she was keen for all young students to use ipads:

> Year Four children [eight or nine years old] have used them in maths lessons and reception children have played some maths and phonics games... Year Ones [four or five-year olds] had them in their religious education lesson... If you walk around the school, there's a child somewhere or a group using the iPad, which is what I want to see.[14]

Young children as young as four and five are being trained to use a technical device that re-wires our brains into specific pathways. Whilst this may be a more natural thing for the 'Digital Natives' (those children born into a digital world), there surely must be a common-sense understanding of when, where, and how to interact with such technologies. Young children wandering around school, or elsewhere, immersed in a non-physical reality will find themselves developing specific mental traits. It is reported that since 1970, the radius of outdoor play activity for a child has shrunk by ninety per cent. Instead of running around outside in nature, children are now prone to be more indoors or more sedentary with their technological gadgets.[15] Similarly, in the UK the National Trust produced a report where they coined the term 'nature deficit disorder' to show how the younger generation has become dissociated with the natural world (it is not a medical condition, just a mental one).

Despite these obvious worrying trends, there are other more

positive aspects regarding how younger people are interacting and making use of technologies.* School classrooms are increasingly incorporating the larger, global world into their midst. Yet at the same time what is needed is a shift from fixed one-size-fits-all curriculums and awful standardized testing. We need more self-education and auto-didactic pursuits — with vision, innovation, and creativity. The imagination needs to be given wings to fly and not be clipped and abolished from the learning environment. Some of our best minds have been daydreamers, famously including Einstein. Imagination is one of the values that can push back the influence of the Wounded Mind. The mental pathogen fears creativity and unscripted innovation.

Compulsory schooling loves the indoctrination effect of boredom. Long-time teacher John Taylor Gatto noted that in schools, boredom had become the common condition — also amongst the schoolteachers. We are left with this chilling yet prescient prediction for fifty years into the future, made by the science fiction writer Isaac Asimov in relation to the 1964 New York World's Fair:

> Even so, mankind will suffer badly from the disease of boredom, a disease spreading more widely each year and growing in intensity. This will have serious mental, emotional and sociological consequences, and I dare say that psychiatry will be far and away the most important medical specialty in 2014. The lucky few who can be involved in creative work of any sort will be the true elite of mankind, for they alone will do more than serve a machine.[16]

And for the rest, dumbed by the mental pathogen that is compulsory schooling, they shall wander through life as ghosts in the modern machine. And this shall be our metaphysical malaise.

---

* See my earlier book *The Phoenix Generation: A New Era of Connection, Compassion & Consciousness* (2014).

Chapter Five

The Metaphysical Malaise

'The real tragedy of our time lies not so much in the unprecedented external events themselves as in the unprecedented ethical destitution and spiritual infirmity which they glaringly reveal.'

Paul Brunton

'If the individual is not truly regenerated in spirit,
society cannot be either,
for society is the sum total of individual
in need of redemption.'

C.G. Jung

The modern world seeks to evade the richness of the inner life. As has been shown through our systems of schooling, the immature child grows up yet is not nurtured within. The alienation and rage that can develop through the forced mental conditioning of our younger years finds release into a material world. The dominant narrative fostered upon malleable minds renders them consumers. School campuses are rigged with vending machines and drinks companies vie for monopoly markets and a captive audience that they hope will remain brand-loyal for the rest of their lives. As trained consumers, they are encouraged not to think about such things. As a result, they are left as sitting ducks for the deluge that is the slick marketing of the modern era. And within this educational morass so many of us are trained to believe in the fantasy that we are a living species within a non-living universe, and that we can go about as 'business as usual', and with a worldly indifference.

This is the myth that the solid, material world is 'out there' and we are just separate bodies wondering around within it. This mentality places everything at a distance from us, believing that there is *us* and then there is the external world. This belief system has been rendered into a civilizational pathology that Forbes refers to as the *wetiko* virus. It has been responsible for humanity feeling it has the right, or even duty, to conquer and control the world around us. From this has come brutal colonization and genocide. Yet in doing so, we have orphaned ourselves not only from our life environments but also from our own sense of self. We have alienated ourselves and become a discontented species. We have been handed – or rather, conditioned with – a view of the world that is dry and barren, like rusting metal in a wasteland. A world of separate objects may have seemed like a good idea at the time, yet in the long term it is not life-affirming. We only have to take a look at the world today to see that things are not going well (to put it mildly).

There is no doubt that we are living in an age of extreme contradictions where opposing trends appear to exist side by side. It is a world where individuals take greater care of their bodies and are obsessed by diet and health fads, whilst obesity is an epidemic. We live amidst a paradoxical combination of playfulness and fear, of fun and anxiety, of euphoria and unease. It can be said that:

> A week without a world sensation hardly exists. Our newspapers give us in a single issue what was once the history of a whole month. Their pages dismay and distract us with reports of new crises that follow each other rhythmically; they tense and strain our nerves with pictures of depressed markets or oppressed mankind; they narrow our eyes with stories of swift changes. The situation is already dramatic enough and would be fantastic were it not so tragic too... The real tragedy of our time lies not so much in the unprecedented external events themselves as in the unprecedented ethical destitution and spiritual infirmity which they glaringly reveal.[1]

This quote adequately describes our current situation and yet it was published in 1952. The author, Paul Brunton, goes on to say that, 'When a materialistic civilization becomes outwardly impressive but remains inwardly impoverished, when political relations become an elaborate façade for hiding the spiritually empty rooms behind them, menacing problems are sure to appear on every side.'[2] Brunton remains as starkly correct in his analysis, as it was for his own time. The result is that 'menacing problems' are indeed appearing on every side: political corruption and ineptitude; economic manipulations; national aggression and politically-motivated warfare; refugee crises; human torture and suffering; capitalist greed; corporate corruption; aggravated social unrest; religious and moral intolerance; increased displays of psychopathic behaviour (private individuals and authority figures); blatant propaganda; environmental degradation; ecological ignorance; spiritual destitution, and the rest.

In a period of increased instability – of horror, terror and suffering – it is no surprise that despairing energies encircle the world. This is the playground that feeds the Wounded Mind. In the terms used by Rudolf Steiner (Chapter Two), this is exactly the environmental conditions that Ahriman intended: a materialistic worldview; a dead, mechanical universe; a dominant economic agenda for social systems; rising nationalism; separatist party politics; the rise of religious fundamentalism; and the dominance of a dry, intellectual culture (as in our sciences). It almost seems as if the *wetiko*-Ahriman-predator pathogen has been successful.

The result is that many people have become 'spiritually numbed' by what they see occurring in the world, and feel that only a similar harsh, physical response can be effective. The words 'mystical' and 'spiritual' remain vague and ethereal. People have always depended on language to bring guidance and nourishment. Yet in this mental environment, words are but skeletal traces of the real flesh. The crisis of our times has clarified little and succeeds in confusing almost everything for the rest of us. There is nowhere to turn in public for finding the truth – virtually nothing to believe in for the present and too much uncertainty for the future. The result of this is that many people have doubts that they don't know how to deal with, and these are building up within their minds like a pathological infection.

An Absence of Meaning

Those people whose metaphysical grounding has been replaced by a materialistic one will never perceive the truth inherent in our potential for internal, spiritual development. Yet although they do not consider these truths, it does not remove them from their sphere of operation. It is a sign of our times that so many people are preoccupied with the external circumstances of their lives that they neglect, or do not even sense, their higher longing. This can be understood when we recognize that this evasion or neglect of the inner self is an intentional act from the collective psychosis. As I have said, the Wounded Mind fears its own disclosure. It seeks to remain undetected, and like a form of mental cancer, to be accepted within the general body as a 'healthy cell' — as *one of us*. But this 'mind' is not *ours*. And we need to remember this, always.

At the same time there remains a sense, a feeling, of something lacking or missing within us. Unfortunately, this need has been met by the consumerist marketplace. There is a great deal of compensation for this lack through 'quick fix' guruism; that is, costly paid retreats, so-called spiritual counselling, and 'life coaching' mentorship. Yet these are like fast-food remedies for a deeper hunger. The real struggle today is rather between the material perspective on life and that of the inner, spiritual dimension. Many of the events occurring in the world are manifestations of some of the same issues existing within ourselves. That is, the anger and negativity we see so much of in the world is a projection from the collective interior state of humanity. We can manifest both the dream or the nightmare, and we share in its waking state. Being physically mature is not enough; we also need to be emotionally, intellectually, and spiritually mature. As I said, we grow in years throughout our schooling, but we fail to grow or be nurtured within.

Our cultures and societies are in disequilibrium because they seek to be governed by artificial laws that ignore the timeless wisdom of the ancient understanding. Those who rule our world often claim to pursue higher values, yet they say very little or nothing about the existence of spiritual higher powers that are as much a part of our cosmic reality as ourselves. This mentality promotes a short-sighted, myopic worldview whereby everything that exists in our perspective is all there is and all that we need to be concerned with. It is a mentality that promotes fear, defence and attack, rather than a welcoming, embracing vision.

Our societies do not consider human purpose and the meaning of our existence. They lead us to live by working, to enjoy through diversions, and to eventually die with debt and taxes. The world is protected by the personal interests of power. There is no fairness or equity in this lopsided arrangement. Conferences of peace are based on compromise and not compassion. Trade is based on strength rather than collaboration. Power and politics are at war with each other and do so beyond the reach of accountability. The real powers that run our world are now invisible, intangible, and almost unknown were it not at the same time so pervasive and dangerous. There is a resurgence of the illegitimate, surging through our black markets, offshores, and dark networks. Dark pathways will always emerge and grow in the places where the light is flickering without focus or intent. We 'are witnessing the emergence of a low-profile world that defies conceptualization because it is forbidden, repressed; it is illegal or illegitimate, or both at the same time.'[3]

Today's so-called modern cultures are increasingly fragmented, or like liquid streams, that can no longer be accurately identified or navigated by the old signs, symbols, and meanings. Modern life has, to some degree, started to dissolve in order to re-assemble. This may indeed be a part of the needed cathartic process we have to pass through upon this planet. Yet the collective Wounded Mind is fighting back with all its reserves, and this disturbance is manifesting across the planet. A feature of our current times is that new ways of thinking and behaviour have not yet fully materialized into the present order of things.

Our relationships are now more fluid than ever, forming through connections, networks, and distances, rather than relying on personal, physical acquaintance. Because of the rapid growth of networks, we are seeing a shift in how our cultures have begun to separate the essential from the peripheral. Peripheral notions of speed, efficiency, economy and power have taken full priority over the essential elements of personal happiness, meaning and inner growth. What is essential gets left out of everyday 'ordinary lives.' That which now constitutes our 'daily life' is void of the questions of metaphysical meaning. Any notion of the spiritual, or the metaphysical, is deemed outside of daily life, and we are taught – or conditioned – not to allow it to enter. In other words, we should not let anything that is 'other' – otherworldly or transcendental – replace the responsibility of our social daily grind. As Chantal Delsol notes, 'the faces of God and the institutions safeguarding transcendence are themselves no longer meaningful.'[4]

Our societies often make political declarations to promote what they decide to be 'social happiness.' Or at least they make public gestures in this direction. Yet our political institutions have no genuine models for this, for their dominant mindset is overruled by a form of psychosis. Social 'happiness' is whatever fits into the particular dominant belief system of the age. And as we have seen, this dominant belief, or narrative, has been hijacked by the Wounded Mind. The truth of it is that as a collective society we have no lasting image of happiness. As a consequence of this, our personal lives are in danger of becoming now less about actual experience and more about the data we leave as trails behind us. We have entered another struggle – another social fray – where we battle between the transparency of our private, inner lives and our public identity.

Our Identity & Self

More and more of us are increasingly offering our private life for public consumption – our photos, our song choices, favourite videos, new romantic engagements, marriage announcements, and all the rest. At the same time, that which we can call our genuine, inner self gets covered over as if we fear what others may see. We willingly make our so-called 'private' lives public, yet we shy away from exposing, or even acknowledging, our true inner life – that quiet, inner voice that whispers to us in the dark. *A voice in the dark whispered to me saying, 'There is no such thing as a voice whispering in the dark.'*

Our joy of attention, of being noticed, is offset (or bought out) at the expense of personal disclosure. We parade what we consider to be our 'selves' because we now feel connected to others like never before. Yet can we sustain this sense of human connectivity at a more fundamental, essential level? We must be careful that the need for genuine connection is not replaced by a public collective mind that regulates and traumatizes itself. From blogs, social media posts, personal videos and phone images, we are lulled into a public performance – a public exhibitionism – unparalleled in our social history. Secrecy is now seen as something anti-social. *'What, you don't want to tell me your age, or who you were dating last night?'* Schoolchildren are more likely to be bullied online than at school. And it is not only the kids who suffer from online bullying, or the 'trolls' as they are also referred to. From celebrities to everyday folk, we are all susceptible to the cyber molestation and inhumane treatment that are manifesting in these modern times. The online platform – the internet, the world wide web – doesn't steal our humanity, it reflects it. This medium doesn't so much get inside us as it shows what's inside of us. The Wounded Mind wants the human shadow to come on out and be revealed.

According to Jung, the psychological 'shadow' is the under-developed and undesirable aspects of ourselves that we try to keep hidden away. And yet there are times when we are unable to hold it at bay, or unconsciously wish for it to manifest. We possess a tremendous imagination for doing good as well as evil, and this can be a finer line than we realize. As the aphorism states, *the road to hell is paved with good intentions.* We need to exercise the capacity to detect and acknowledge those unconscious desires, feelings, and thoughts that exist within us. If we don't, then the psychosis, the mental pathogen that seeks entry into the depths of our minds, may manifest them on our behalf. We are seeing the consequences of this now throughout the world. American psychologist Rollo May once wrote: 'Our age is one of transition, in which the normal channels for utilizing the daemonic are denied; and such ages tend to be times when the daemonic is expressed in its most destructive form.'[5]

In short, we need to be extremely mindful in these times about what's inside of us. Our minds – our thinking and consciousness – are a target and have been for a long time. In the last century this has become more evident, more public. The modern psychosis that is the Wounded Mind has been responsible for atrocities on a global scale, from warfare to genocide; from the Holocaust and its regime of systematic torture and rationalized slaughter, from modern day detention camps (Guantanamo Bay) to tyrannical 'ethnic cleansing'. Somewhere along the way we began to lose our souls.

Soul Loss

We have become increasingly stuck in modern times within our own stories around psychological need and a 'loss of self'. Perhaps what we also need to acknowledge is that some of us are suffering from soul loss. Shamanic healer Sandra Ingerman says that most people have more than one part of themselves missing. Different traumas are experienced throughout our lives, causing pieces of our essence to leave us. According to Ingerman, one meaning of soul is to mean simply our vital essence. Thus, the experience of soul loss (or loss of vital essence) may occur due to trauma or shock; a loss or abuse, or to survive a painful experience such as physical or sexual abuse. People who experience soul loss frequently have the feeling of being fragmented; not whole or completely 'in' themselves. They feel as if an essential part of them is missing. They may clinically be diagnosed as 'dissociated'. Depression is another symptom of soul loss. Soul loss can be associated with the traumas of modern life – fear, terror (warfare), incest or rape, domestic abuse. These are all the external stresses that modern life creates.

Similarly, John Bradshaw uses the term *toxic shame* which he sees as a form of spiritual bankruptcy; alienation from the self, causing it to be 'otherated', and so we turn to external sources to fill this internal void. This is soul loss by another name. Bradshaw notes that: 'Our society is highly addictive. We have 60 million sexual abuse victims. Possibly 75 million lives are seriously affected by alcoholism, with no telling how many more through other drugs...

Over 15 million families are violent. Some 60% of women and 50% of men have eating disorders. We have no actual data on work addiction or sexual addictions. I saw a recent quotation that cited 13 million gambling addicts.'[6] This is clearly a toxic social problem.

Carl Jung also made a reference to soul loss in his psychological work. According to psychotherapist Robert Francis Johnson,

> This loss of soul Jung speaks of is manifested in our culture by the crises we are all facing (increased drug use, violence, moral and emotional numbness) and our attempt to solve moral and spiritual questions by electing wounded leaders who promise economic answers.[7]

It is interesting that Johnson refers to 'wounded leaders' here, who seek our compliance through the language of greed ('economic answers'). Perhaps it would also be accurate to say, leaders who are infected with and fully manifest the Wounded Mind. Similarly, prominent Jungian analyst Marie von Franz writes that:

> Soul loss can be observed today as a psychological phenomenon in the everyday lives of the human beings around us. Loss of soul appears in the form of a sudden onset of apathy and listlessness; the joy has gone out of life, initiative is crippled, one feels empty, everything seems pointless.[8]

Is this not a description of many people's lives? Apathy, listlessness, a feeling of a pointless, joyless life? Is this not the result of being under the sway of a psychosis that has distorted our perception of reality? I am reminded of a saying from Jesus Christ where he says: 'For what is a man profited, if he shall gain the whole world, and lose his own soul?'

It is time for each of us to collect back our lost pieces and remember why we were born into this world. We are in need of a metaphysical response.

Where is the Metaphysical?

Any society or civilization that does not recognize the human as a spiritual being will fall short in its accomplishments. We simply cannot allow ourselves to fall short — not in the long run, at least. Yet recognition of the human as a spiritual being will not come from the world first, and definitely not from our social-cultural-political institutions. It will first come only from the individual. And it is from here that genuine change must be nurtured. Now is a crucial time for managing our psychological, emotional, and physical states. We may be uncertain about the future, yet we have the technologies to radically transform our age into something unprecedented. We have both external technologies as well as what I call 'technologies of the soul'. What we *are*, we transmit to others. If we manifest the *wetiko* virus — the mental pathogen — through our relations with those around us, then this feeds into the collective Wounded Mind. We are compelled not only to be mindful, but crucially to be both *sensible* and *soul-ful*.

On a practical level, the number of people around the world who have been awoken by the world crisis to seek the inner life are not the majority. We can say that at present there exists a metaphysical malaise. Those people who aspire for inner self-development — who reach out for the Truth — are still too few. However, a majority was never needed. There are enough.

We are engaged in a profound moment on the human species' path. Whether we recognize it or not, we are each living and participating in a reality that exists upon spiritual and metaphysical principles. That's the bottom line. We can choose to participate in this metaphysical reality consciously and willingly, or to drift through this reality unbeknownst to the forces that impel us. Right now, our life is about recognizing this choice, and whether we act upon it. It will not be easy, given all the obstacles that our psychosis-ridden governing systems will throw at us. And yet it must be a force of unwavering inner commitment and genuine self-trust.

We must choose our freedom from within. The real site of freedom can only be within us — our inner self — and it is to this that we must place our trust. I shall speak more about this in the final part of the book. However, before we arrive there, we must continue the journey through the external world and to observe how the

Wounded Mind is being manifested. We are urged to step through the unreal world and to dip our toes into the hypermodern condition of our lives. Welcome to Part Two.

Part Two

THE UNREAL WORLD

Part Two examines how our technological cultures emerged from a post-modern condition into what I will refer to as the 'hypermodern'. In the following chapters I critique post-modernity; specifically, I discuss how features of hypermodern-technological cultures are under the sway of the Wounded Mind. I examine the cultures of spectacle, entertainment, narcissism, abstraction, catastrophe, freedom, war and insecurity and how these are being formed by this mental psychosis and how it is shaping the new world coming into being today.

Chapter Six

Our Hypermodern Condition

'The challenge of modernity is to live without illusions and without becoming disillusioned.'

Antonio Gramsci

'Once upon a time, all roads led to Rome; now all of them lead through shops.'

Zygmunt Bauman

At all times in human history people have felt uncertain of the future and somewhat lost in the present. This is the predicament of human nature and society. Nothing is, or can be, fully known. In each epoch we consider life to be more or less stable, whilst the truth of it is that we are always participating in fluid history. In the long-term view, we are in constant transition and movement. It is only the limited perspective granted to us within a human lifespan that creates the static, myopic view. Yet there is actually something different about our cultural moment now that is affecting the situation, which I put down to the clash of two epochs – the outgoing and the incoming. Specifically, the more advanced nations of the world are moving into a period of highly-advanced technology, with machine learning (a.k.a. machine intelligence), algorithms, digital networks and global technological infrastructures, automation and robotics, digital/3D manufacturing, nanotechnology, and biological engineering being some of these key features. Within these aspects exist an array of many more nuanced variables. Our understanding of a linear world has also shifted into that of an asymmetrical or irregular landscape.

We live within a world of chance, of unlimited connections, perturbations, and unknown or uncertain consequences. It is like a mighty algorithm that acts in ways beyond our human perception. Modern life is nothing like it was in past epochs. Today, across the planet, we are a networked, nonlinear, asymmetrical mass of people who are projecting their individual minds upon the global stage. Today, the issue of control – that is, social management, is more dominant than ever.

In past ages, social management was enforced through control over the physical body. As is historically recorded, it was the custom in past centuries to punish an offender by public display. This may have taken the form of being tied to the wooden stocks in the main town or village square, or paraded through the streets. The extreme form of this technique was public execution, through various cruel means. This had the effect of warning others against rebellious acts or anti-social behaviour. Given that in contemporary times our societies no longer operate along these crude means, the channels of power are more subtle. Principally, they operate through managing how people think, which then regulates and normalizes their behaviour. The age of Enlightenment that prefigured the modern age, was the precursor to the emergence of bureaucratic and disciplinary forms of control paraded as social norms. Techniques were then devised and employed through modern societies to produce normalized and standardized behaviour in order to create a socially managed populace. Such a managed populace would be more adapted for regulated forms of mechanical, industrial employment, which would be largely factory based.

The modern collective mind has been adapted into its own mechanism of control, which now operates principally through modes of communication. Recently, the mainstream broadcast media has been able to achieve through subtle means, and in our private spaces, what the executioner was forced to do in public through heavy instruments. The Wounded Mind is obsessive about social control and its expression in 'socially responsible behaviour'. To enact this, a consortium of institutions has grown up that structures our contemporary societies and gives it a specific shape. This is the shape of perceived human autonomy that in actual fact develops increased social dependency. Our credit liberty to go out and have purchase power to enjoy the things in life, is at the same time our chains of enslavement to a system that we literally buy into. The Wounded Mind seeks our willing obedience through clever strategies of voluntary compliance.

The values and concepts of morality that we take to be our own are actually imposed upon us externally, although now by more subtle means: less of the public punishment and more of the media messages. The collective Wounded Mind attempts to find new channels for *giving us its mind,* and to do this it needs us – the recipient – to be as compliant as possible. Modern life has therefore been preparing us, and continues to do so, to become compliant automatons. Everyday life is now regulated to the point of a military regime. When we arrive at airports we are shown – and then told – where to put our feet, how to lift our arms, and when to shuffle obediently through the scans. We are uncomfortably jostled through an elaborate labyrinth of technical humiliations and physical constraints. The result is that we become mentally submissive, quietly praying within for the ordeal to be over. Modern life has been characterized by a range of pseudo-myths that we have come to live by, inhabited by a mass of norms, values, and regulations.

Our era has now become one of increasing 'unreality' to the point where it has become an age of superstition. I'm not referring to the superstitions of the metaphysical or the 'spooky' realm. Rather, I refer to the superstitions where one clings to worn-out belief systems, cultural behaviour and those odd quirks that once held meaning. These superstitions are now the old-hat ideologies that no longer work for us, and yet our authorities and power structures cling to them and drag our societies further into the blurred realms of unreality. The forces of power in our world have turned their insatiable greed into a ghost ship, and like a Mary Celeste it drifts across our watery landscapes bringing uncertainty and its malignant sister, dread. The Wounded Mind seeks to deliberately cut our connection to the Real. The result of this is that modern life as we know it, in the West especially, has become fluid to the extent that it has been referred to as the *hypermodern.*[*]

---

[*] See the work of theorist Gilles Lipovetsky.

Our Hypermodern Societies

Contemporary everyday lives seem to be fascinated by the super-fluous, the frivolous, the trivial spectacle. We are cajoled and entertained, allowed public expressions of opinion; and yet some-where beneath all this is the feeling of being spectators at a circus. As philosopher Gilles Lipovetsky says – 'Hypercapitalism, hyper-class, hyperpower, hyperterrorism, hyperindividualism, hyper-market, hypertext – is there anything that isn't "hyper"?'[1] It seems that there is an explosion of the 'hyper', which also includes its own excess – manic consumption; drugs in athletics; extreme sports; violence, terrorism, school killings; anorexia and obesity; compul-sions and addictions. It is in the hyper where extreme contra-dictions come together as opposing trends. As previously mentioned, we are living in a time where individuals take greater care of their bodies and are obsessed by diet and health fads, while obesity is an epidemic. The trauma of the Wounded Mind keeps us unbalanced through ongoing contradictions.

These extreme contradictions get played out in our everyday habits and obsessions. Strict diet regimes with their expensive bottles of vitamins and supplements are mirrored in the extreme by people who fall into anorexia or bulimia. The other extreme, of course, is the nosedive into fast food, over-consumption, and now prolific obesity. Modern societies are obsessed with the twin evils of excessive slimness (such as in fashion models) and ignorant obesity (as in 'Super Size me'). Our minds are targeted and influenced by trendy-seeming fashions that are little else than superficial drapery. Our so-called advanced cultures promote gimmicky fashion around the logistics and trappings of seduction. We have been seduced into play and on to the playing field, whether willingly or through whimsy resistance. Seduction is delivered to us and we con-summate the offering in our participation. We are seduced by the cult of the 'new' in which a built-in-obsolescence pervades our marketplace of goods. It is the fabrication of false needs, increasing desires, and the gadget-ization of our lives.

The hyper of hypermodernity encourages the expression and

manifestation of individual desires; these can easily be the paths to pseudo self-fulfilment, as well as the array of means for gaining social status. The private sphere has spilled over into the public domain, and an age of spectacle now entertains us through a circus of triviality. Narcissus has been born again as a celebrated public figure – hedonistic, playful, and superficially liberating. We revel in the euphoric energies of self-emancipation ratified with the emptiness of modern ideologies. Narcissus is now in love with a masculine body that assaults its power over what it falsely conceives to be lesser bodies and minds. Cruel sexual and psychological harassment is now an assault on modern life. The search for the authentic 'me' has morphed into the #MeToo. Our personalities are destabilizing, just as they would through trauma where the mind compartmentalizes experiences.

The Destabilized Personality

The individual is publicly encouraged to take possession of their own life, as if they are master of themselves. And yet this possession of life can only take place within set parameters of limited freedom that includes attachments, consumerism, hedonism, and economic-dependency. Our lives are lived longer, yet upon ever more unstable foundations. What we are seeing in the world is an increase in pathological behaviour alongside ennui and boredom. It appears that through 'its operations of technocratic normalization and the loosening of social bonds, the hypermodern age simultaneously manufactures order and disorder, subjective independence and dependence, moderation and excess'.[2] In this way, our modern cultures seem desperate to normalize happiness. It can be coached to us by lifestyle gurus, or contained in exotic vacations, or gained through meditative retreats. Happiness, we are told, is attainable in the marketplace – we only have to work out a path through all the available offerings in order to reach this goal. A balanced life can be sought, bought, and paid for. And in this, we can feel relieved. Everything is available, it seems.

With the possibility of engaging in ever more abstract lifestyles, we are open to the increased destabilizing of the personality. The 'personality' has become a fragile thing; it is analysed, scrutinized, and criticized through social media; it is shared or thrown around excessively through photo-sharing sites, and the rest. In the age of hyper-reproduction, our personalities are being copied feverously and left vulnerable to moral, as well as cyber, hackers. A sense of unease and inadequacy is creeping in and is excessively present. This can lead to the potential for an epidemic of psychological vulnerability. Which child will be the next victim of cyber-bullying? Who will be next to take their life as the unseen pressure mounts? The Wounded Mind can turn on an individual so fast that there is no time to process the situation. As Sebastien Charles writes,

> Hypermodern individuals are both better informed and more destructured, more adult and more unstable, less ideological and more in thrall to changing fashions, more open and more easy to influence, more critical and more superficial, more sceptical and less profound.[3]

On having a platform for global exposure, we demand recognition; our sense of happiness and worth is framed by this recognition – of our rights, our sexuality, our identity, etc. And to be denied this recognition is one of the things that annoys us most. The Wounded Mind likes nothing better than for individuals to air their dirty laundry in public, and to engage in squabbles that fill the front-page news. This collective 'wetiko mind' might be forgiven for being diagnosed as bipolar, wavering between its euphoric highs and depressed lows. This is directly a response to the emotional stimuli that it is fed, primarily through mainstream culture.

Our modern gossip-fuelled cultures, deprived of transcendent truths, have become a permanent playground for resentments and in-fighting. In a world of global technologies of communication, the Wounded Mind gleefully seems to want to parade dysfunctional behaviour across the front headlines. And yet there is no real lasting, sustainable future in this. Trauma requires its catharsis, its cleansing. In order to move into a more aligned and agreeable future, we first need to cast our shadows out of us – a collective species-wide exorcism, perhaps? The psychologist Jung was well aware that our issues stemmed from the psychosis of our collective minds. He stated in various ways that the modern 'cultural mind' exhibited an alarming degree of dissociation and psychological confusion. And as if mirroring the *wetiko* pathogen, Jung also noted that,

> He [modern man] is blind to the fact that, with all his rationality and efficiency, he is possessed by powers beyond his control. The gods and demons have not disappeared at all, they have merely got new names. They keep him on the run with restlessness, vague apprehensions, psychological complications, an invincible need for pills, alcohol, tobacco, dietary and other hygienic systems – and above all, with an impressive array of neuroses.[4]

Jung was well aware that our modern lives fostered a rootlessness that produced also a lack of meaning; something which he referred to as a form of 'soul-sickness' which our societies had not yet begun to comprehend. Jung observed that,

> People will do anything, no matter how absurd, in order to avoid facing their own souls. They will practice Indian yoga and all its exercises, observe a strict regimen of diet, learn theosophy by heart, or mechanically repeat mystic texts from the literature of the whole world – all because they cannot get on with themselves and have not the slightest faith that anything useful could ever come out of *their* souls.[5]

The modern world of hyper-everything appears to have a liking for eating the human soul; some sort of fast-food ethereal snack. Such a condition needs to change in order for us to re-vision the future.

The Future Now?

It could be that what we are currently witnessing is the manifestation and expression of our collective shadows being paraded publicly. Some of this is coming out within our politics with the obvious signs of corruption, bullying, arrogance, ignorance, and some downright nastiness. We have educated adults bickering like children in the global playground, and it shows a clear regression of the human soul-spirit. Global humanity is a sensitive – and potentially sensible – organism. And yet we are living at a time of immense psycho-stimulation. We are also presented with an almost infinite complexity of phenomena which are overwhelming our senses and capacity for balanced perception. In its place we are having a socially constructed and manipulated perception fostered upon us in the form of social discipline and collective obedience. We are right in the middle of a time of intense 'enforced socialization'.

The future that awaits us appears greatly more complex than anyone could have foreseen. We are faced with unprecedented uncertainty about the future, and yet we have the technologies to radically transform our age into something extraordinary. In a sense, we are building bridges to the future without asking, or knowing, how wide the river is. The future is both compelling and compels us – and so we race ahead. Within this uncertain and rapid fluidity there is little consideration for our spiritual, or soulful, well-being. Jung came to the realization later in his life that 'spiritual adjustment', as he called it, was *the* problem of our modern epoch.

Our contemporary condition (we may also call it the 'crisis of our times') has little clarity or collective vision for the future. There is seemingly nowhere in our culture to turn for finding the truth. The result of this is that most people have doubts that are accumulating within their minds like a pathological infection, obscuring their vision and sanity.

The visible, global disagreements – the struggles and conflicts – are an expression of what already exists in our mental and emotional states. In other words, the true war is the psychological one, and this is being manifested outside of us and upon the world stage. In a time of increased instability – of terror and suffering – it is no surprise that negative energies are ever-present in the world. The result is that many people have become 'spiritually numbed' by what they see occurring around them. Yet in some people, the awareness of an inner lack has become more acute, and that some inner satisfaction is a necessity. Throughout modernity – including 'post' and 'hyper' modernity especially – it was unfashionable to be intensely serious about matters of the soul. Light-hearted and experimental spiritualism was accepted, with New Age, crystal consumerism, and yoga groupings being the zeitgeist – the fashion of the age. And now we find ourselves out upon the vast waters without a captain or internal satellite for guidance. Without proper internal guidance, we are each susceptible to the external impacts from the mass of life.

Modern life bombards us with constant suggestions from collective group-think and consensus opinions; from social forms and institutions, and from conventions and values that shape and discipline our conditioned thinking. Everybody, to a greater or lesser degree, lives within this collective life that influences them. The degree of a person's own independence is relative to their own inner guiding strength. If a person gives away too much of their capacity for thinking and reflection, then they also lose their independent will, and this makes it more difficult to break away from the collective pull of crowd mentality. We each basically have two forms of submission open to us: we are free to be a servant of our higher self or a slave to our lower nature. And yet the power to independently choose has often been blurred by the stress of our lives.

Modern living, especially within dense urban metropolises, as well as within poverty-stricken neighbourhoods, severely pollutes our psychological states of mind, as well as affecting our nervous systems. We now have more neurotic and psychologically-imbalanced people in our world than at any time in history. The Wounded Mind is a global phenomenon. It is imperative that each person learns to live at a pace and rhythm that suits them best, and to resist getting pulled into the collective trauma that seeks to absorb us, heart and soul. At present, a disorder of the inner world is being continually fed by the assault of media-driven trivialities, globally-projected disarray, and a great energy of uncertainty. We need to become aware of the absurd spectacles, as I discuss in the next chapter.

Chapter Seven

The Spectacle of the Absurd

'Two centuries ago when a great man appeared, people looked for God's purpose in him; today we look for his press agent.'

Daniel Boorstin

'Appearance on the television screen is the only substitute for transcendence, and all in all it's a satisfying substitute.'

Umberto Eco

The modern spirit believes itself – or so we have been told – to have been born under the sign of the pursuit of happiness. We deem it a right to seek satisfactions, whether they be true or not, because we don't wish to be reminded of our lack. Or rather, we wish not to sense, to *feel*, the traces of the Wounded Mind. To compensate for this, modern society has worked hard at creating spectacles to keep us entertained, from media, news, events, sport, and the rest. As social critic Neil Postman famously stated – 'Americans are the best entertained and quite likely the least well-informed people in the Western world.'[1] Yet that accolade no longer belongs to Americans alone – the rest of us in many so-called 'advanced societies' have joined the club.

In the second part of the twentieth century, sociologist Christopher Lasch observed that modern society had shifted into 'societies of the self' where self-interests, self-concern, and self-love were the dominant factors. He noted that we had become our own narcissistic cultures. Luckily for him, he was not around to witness the arrival of online social media and the 'selfie' craze. Previously, the feeling of 'something lacking' and the spectres of war (Vietnam, Korea, Cold War, etc.) is likely to have compelled people to crave for an illusion of well-being and personal safety. It was a longing for some form of psychic security, whether it be a fantasy or not, so long as it provided a safe harbour. Since then, people the world over have become more interested in their 'private performances' in a way that cultivates an odd form of mystical self-attention.

Lasch, who published his seminal work *The Culture of Narcissism: American Life in An Age of Diminishing Expectations* in the 1970s, described contemporary culture as featuring, 'the intense fear of old age and death, altered sense of time, fascination with celebrity, fear of competition, decline of the play spirit, deteriorating relations between men and women.'[2] It doesn't seem that much has changed in the intervening half-century. Lasch saw these features as describing a state of mind where the world appears as a mirror of the self. Our overt performances of the 'grandiose self' was just a cover-up of intense feelings of emptiness and inauthenticity. These inner stirrings were thus fuelling the 'self-growth' industry, which Lasch also viewed as being superficially optimistic and radiating a sense of resignation rather than hope:

> Having no hope of improving their lives in any of the ways that matter, people have convinced themselves that what matters is psychic self-improvement: getting in touch with their feelings, eating health food ... immersing themselves in the wisdom of the East... Harmless in themselves, these pursuits, elevated to a programme and wrapped in the rhetoric of authenticity and awareness, signify a retreat from politics and a repudiation of the recent past.[3]

The genuine path of self-development is always one of hope, clarity, and wisdom. It is also anathema to the mental virus that seeks the reverse – a passive, compliant mind. Rather than deny access to means of self-discovery, the corrupted culture made a smarter choice. It provided exactly what was sought – all neatly packaged as false gold.

Modern consumer cultures give us endless choice and possibility; an array of pretty indulgences, absorbing pursuits, etc. Yet rather than delivering the essential, these serve to mask an inner void by providing forms of social banality. Personal and social banality and boredom is now glossed over by civilized distractions. Plagued by anxiety and feelings of insecurity, the average person today wishes for peace of mind rather than seeking the vague promise of spiritual fulfilment. This 'peace of mind' is provided by coming into the fold of the collective 'consensus mind'. This need to seek safety is exacerbated today by social and global conditions that are often manipulated to provide this function (see Chapter Nine). The need for self-absorption is also a response mechanism that works to insulate a person against the raw brutalities occurring on the street, across the world, and elsewhere. The brutal realities of poverty, racism, violence and injustice are filtered out of the bubble that we insulate ourselves with. Our modern societies today also serve to detach and disassociate us from the Machiavellian manoeuvres of the political elite. This state of mental apathy and disassociation is more a characteristic of the Wounded Mind than it is any specific medical condition.

Playful mainstream media pretends to give us scrutiny and investigative reporting when really all it gives are information-makeovers. This is not to be confused with genuine investigations and self-examination, which still thankfully exist, albeit in the minority. Much of the media today operates along the lines of con-fessional self-disclosure, appealing to people's sense of curiosity. Whereas news, media, and entertainment were previously more descriptive or didactic, today they have veered into popularist exposé and superficial accounting. We witness this in the rise of daytime television shows where screaming families are pitted against one another; or the programmes that offer 'ugly duckling' makeovers. Today we want to pry into the lives of others, whether it be the Osbourne Family show or other pseudo-celebrity reality shows. Our media world is now a grand theatrical performance; a stage upon which illusion thrives and where we welcome the joy of attention.

The Joy of Attention

'Mirror, mirror on the wall, who is the fairest one of all?'

the Queen in 'Snow White and the Seven Dwarfs'

Modern Western cultures are infamous for engaging in scopophilia, or the love of being seen; this is creating a willing, consumer-based mass of people that are happy to be under surveillance. This has now spread to non-Western, developed societies such as South Korea and Japan, whose highly technologized societies have altered historic cultural modes of behaviour.[4] Novelist, essayist and critic Umberto Eco wryly noted that:

> In other words, for the first time in the history of mankind, those who are being spied upon are helping the spies to make their work easier, and gain satisfaction from being observed as they live, even if at times they are behaving like criminals or idiots ... those being spied upon think it's a good thing that their friends, their neighbors, and perhaps their enemies know their most intimate secrets, as this is the only way they feel themselves to be a living and active part of the social body.[5]

To be an 'active part of the social body' has conditioned us into consuming a 'joy of attention'. That is, we want to be noticed, and this desire is bought into at the expense of personal disclosure. We parade what we consider to be our 'selves' because we now have a friend-littered platform in which to perform. This 'alien mind' has persuaded us into personal disclosure and transparency as if it were a good thing.

Transparency on our part is required if we are to have our public revelations. Enhanced visibility – being seen 'out in the open' – also brings us a sense of social recognition, which for some brings a sense of meaning. Again, as Eco notes – 'But perhaps in the so-called liquid society, where people suffer from lack of identity and values, and have no points of reference, the only means for obtaining social recognition is through "being seen" at all costs.'[6] This is especially evident through the modern craze for Reality TV and individuals' desire to be watched, warts and all, by as many viewing spectators as possible – whether it is on *Big Brother*, *I'm a Celebrity Get Me Out of Here*, *The X-Factor*, *Survivor*, or *The Great Bake Off*. To be seen – to be visible – somehow keeps away our modern fear of being ignored.

The rise of the popular 'celebrity culture' is a symptom of our narcissistic desire to be admired, and by more the better. Modern society not only elevates narcissists to prominence, it also promotes and supports narcissistic features within the mainstream. Narcissism is promoted as being an attractive trait. Modern media is rife with narcissism and yet, it seems, we fail to realize that it only makes us more immature and, further, reinforces our dependencies. We can see how the mental pathogen loves and promotes our narcissistic tendencies – it stops us from asking penetrating and revealing questions about the nature of reality. In short, it helps the mental virus to evade detection. We are too enamoured with ourselves to notice its lingering presence within. An anonymous phrase states – *When the gods want to punish us, they make us believe our own advertising*. It could also easily be said that we are made to believe our own fantasies about ourselves. We certainly believe in our entertainments.

What we are given today are branded names and packaged celebrities. The historian Daniel Boorstin famously said that the chief claim to fame of celebrities is their fame itself. That is, the celebrity was a person who had become known for their 'well-knownness'. Boorstin, writing in the 1960s, presciently observed that, 'Celebrity is made by simple familiarity, induced and re-enforced by public means. The celebrity therefore is the perfect embodiment of tautology: the most familiar is the most familiar.'[7] Celebrities are known according to their personality, which is always on show for us, the spectators (or rather, consumers). A synonym for a 'celebrity' is a well-known 'personality' and yet personality comes from 'persona' meaning 'a mask'. Celebrities are just manufactured masks for public consumption. Yet so many people project onto them; they worship, mimic, and even stalk these personalities.

Our spectacle cultures seem to promote fickle talents rather than innate capacity. Like consumables, C-list celebs, from throw-away reality television shows, are themselves thrown away when they no longer appeal to a market audience. Overnight sensations are forgotten overnight, and the one-album manufactured pop groups are discarded for the next one-album pop group. Umberto Eco was being sarcastic when he wrote in one of his newspaper columns that, 'People move from one act of consumption to another in a sort of purposeless bulimia'[8] – yet he had a point.

We are able like never before to fabricate and consume our experiences, and this includes our news, our celebrities, our entertainment, and even our celebrations. We can turn anything into a spectacle. The spectacle beguiles us. We love our Oscars, Golden Globes, Screen Actors' Guild, Grammys, Baftas, MTV music, and the rest of our public award ceremonies. We pride ourselves with glamour and self-appreciation, like going around in the same club patting ourselves on our backs. It is a show, a spectacle, that is totally self-engrossed and self-referential. The shaman don Juan would have had a field day with this type of behaviour. I'm sure that don Juan would also know that being beguiled by spectacle does not nourish one's sense of well-being. Attachment to the spectacle only reinforces a person's sense of being at the mercy of outside forces. Or, in this case, at the mercy of the psychosis that is the Wounded Mind.

A great deal of our modern experience has been deliberately manufactured for the consumption of the collective mindset. Often what we see, hear, and read consists of these artificially produced 'information-events'. It can be said that we take most of our experiences, information – and thus 'knowledge' and opinion – from the theatre of the unreal.

The Theatre of the Unreal

The historian Daniel Boorstin recognized from an early stage that manufactured imagery would come to supplant reality itself. Also, that the media does not act separately from other social institutions, but rather it works in collusion to create an eco-system of simulated events. From this observation, Boorstin coined the term *pseudo-event*. Pseudo-events are a 'new kind of synthetic novelty' that has flooded our modern experience: it possesses the following characteristics – it is not spontaneous but highly planned; it is organized primarily in order to be reported or reproduced; its relation to reality is ambiguous; it is often a self-fulfilling prophecy. Pseudo-events confuse the roles between actors and audience, such as can be seen through Reality TV, which blurs these distinctions. Another popular contemporary form of pseudo-event is the so-called political 'leak'. Such 'leaks' are now used as a regular way of emitting, or transmitting, information; and they are as well-organized as a formal press conference!

Pseudo-events are set-up to dominate our attention over natural, organic events, because they are more dramatic and vivid. By their nature they are easier to disseminate as they are 'media friendly' and are promoted through all the cleverly manipulated online social media channels. They are created to 'go viral' and to appeal to our emotions specifically. They aim to be more attractive and more persuasive than reality itself. They are the things we are subliminally compelled to talk about at work the next day, or in the bars out with friends. We spread them like a virus, because that's exactly what they are. And that is exactly what this mindset is. It is we who give sustenance to the collective mental contagion. And while 'we have given others great power to deceive us, to create pseudo-events, celebrities, and images, they could not have done so without our collaboration'.[9] Pseudo-events are now produced on a mass scale, and they are so implicated into our cultures that we can no longer see them for what they are. Everything now, whether artificial or natural, truth or lie, is intricately woven into the whole machinery of our modern societies.

Life is now like a spectacle sport, and we are all the performers, spectating each other within the same great game.

A Spectacle of Sport

The whole game of sport has been transformed from the spirit of competition to the pockets of commercialization. The transition has occurred over decades, and yet this 'slow boil' phenomenon has been missed by the many. It's easy to see. The signs are everywhere, quite literally. Sport is now image-saturated; its stadiums are filled with famous brand logos and iconic symbols from the consumer's paradise. Top sport stars are now media celebrities that endorse products or release their own line of fashion accessories or perfume. Sport is now big business and show business all rolled into one. It is like a religion, yet instead of the religious buildings there are an array of expensive stadium buildings that litter the globe. This phase of ever-grander stadium building is reminiscent of the explosion in gothic cathedral building during the High and Late Middle Ages in Europe. These state-of-the-art sports stadiums are sites of fervent pilgrimage and ecstatic experiences. From the Roman amphitheatres, where Gladiators fought bloody spectacles, to the huge, domed edifices of today, these constructions house the multitude either in prayer, worship, or ecstasy for the winning side (their temporary gods?). Such spectacles have also been parodied, to great effect, in films such as *The Running Man* (1987), and more recently in *The Hunger Games* book-movie franchise.

Sport is a major component of many people's lives, yet we must distinguish between genuine sport — of independent adventure, courage, commitment, and often team sensibility — and the commercial ventures. Within commercial trappings, the sport celebrity is paid the equivalent of top box-office film stars, and their personal lives are made public and often sensationalized. Yet as we are now increasingly seeing, the spectacle of corporate, commercialized sport is rife with the corruptions we would expect from the *wetiko* virus. In recent years, we've had the FIFA World Cup fraud scandal, the F1 racing corruption scandal, endemic doping in sports, and organized violence. Major sporting clubs are utilized as tax havens by the extreme rich, and sport has now become a playground of extreme finances where spectators spend a fortune to attend. The sporting event is no longer a realm of play but is now largely the domain of *homo corporate* and big bucks. Glamour has been funnelled into extreme rivalry, especially amongst males, with promises of sexualized rewards. And the great sporting reward of teamwork no longer denotes loyalty, as players are regularly traded and swapped (euphemistically called 'transfers') to opposing teams for huge sums.

The notion of play is now coerced into calculated performances, aided by the best team of supporting professionals; from health coaches, psychologists, physiologists, nutritionists, and the rest. What I am trying to say here is that commercial sport has become yet another external spectacle, conjured up by high-ranking bodies to keep the general attention simultaneously entertained and distracted. All this serves to project the collective mind onto external events, which is the central trick of the Wounded Mind. Commercialized sporting events both feed on our emotions as well as feed them in return. We are now in an age of the 'global event', whether it be sporting, musical, or so-called 'charity-based'. Sociology professor Chris Rojek has done extensive research on this phenomenon of the global event, using the World Cup, the Olympics, Live Aid, Burning Man and Mardi Gras as case studies. What he found was that these events are manipulated to incite 'targeted patriotism', or 'targeted solidarity', that creates temporary emotional satisfactions and release. Also, that many such large-scale events are utilized to provide a deliberate, manipulated sense of meaning and belonging.[10]

Rojek's argument is an accurate psychological observation as well as a sociological one. And the message points directly to a strategy of social management. That is, many global events are created to feed people's need for feeling empowered and independent. It also gives them a substitute feeling of engaging in the pursuit of a higher purpose, thus relinquishing the need for any sincere, genuine search. By providing a break from daily routines, and providing a transitory sense of social solidarity, they create a sense of self-validation and personal gratification. In short, such events are made to make us feel good. And it is no accident. Although those involved in organizing the events are by-and-large sincere in what they are doing, they are supported, and often guided, by a system that is intentionally using communication power for social ordering and control. By delivering us our spectacles, the system perpetuates the conditioning of the pathogen that becomes our collective Wounded Mind. And by unconsciously participating and thus validating these forms of social control, we remain as both carriers and deliverers of the wounded mindset. We must be mindful, always, of our individual and collective psychological states.

The world we inhabit, and the future that we will create and leave as a legacy, will depend upon those states that exist within the individual and collective psyche of humanity. We are, quite literally, manifesting a dream in that we project our mental states into a collective reality. The Wounded Mind uses humanity in order to project *its* own state onto the world. And it is driving us mad, in so many ways. We are looking out at the world through a spectral gaze.

Chapter Eight

The Spectral Gaze

'I live in connection with people's emotions, friends' sensations, strangers' reactions, with the information of the flow, the selections produced by social networks... I interpret, receive, feel and participate. I look at the images, I welcome confessions, I eschew insults, I receive emotions, I download songs, I put myself in the hands of the information that Facebook or Twitter favoured and guaranteed, feeding it with "followers" and "likes" by a giant yet exclusive word-of-mouth... I absorb, therefore I know.'

Ezio Mauro, *Babel*

We absorb a multitude of impacts, and then we think 'I know' — but is it through our own minds? Now that we are moving toward a global society it is imperative that we invest our new species body with a sane mind. Nobel laureate Andre Geim has said that:

> We will not survive in our current form. We will evolve into a new one. We are already evolving. The new form is known as the 'global society.' It is a creature infinitely more complex than the old *Homo sapiens*. Human beings are contained within it like the molecules that make up matter. *Homo sapiens* has lasted roughly fifty-thousand years. We will see what this new creature, global society, will become in another fifty-thousand years.[1]

And yet the next fifty-thousand years starts now, today. It will be the present that creates the foundations upon which we build this 'new creature,' as Geim asserts. We have developed the beginnings of our global society and its technological infrastructure. We produce 2.5 exabytes of data every day. That's equivalent to 250,000 Libraries of Congress or the content of 5 million laptops. Every minute of every day 3.2 billion global internet users continue to feed the data banks with 9,722 pins on Pinterest, 347,222 tweets, 4.2 million Facebook likes plus all the other digital data we create by taking pictures and videos, saving documents, opening accounts and more.[2] We have shifted into a self-confessional society where the global stage becomes a platform for promoting public self-exposure. The world 'out there' is becoming another aspect of our personalities. We carelessly, or with great care, extend our individual minds to embrace a larger sphere that is now nothing short of a global mind. Many of us, especially of the younger generations, are quite liberal in publishing details, in text and photos, of our intimate lives. We disclose, and unclothe, ourselves before a largely unknown, collective public. We no longer need the local presence of school bullying (or the guillotine in the town square) as we have accessed the digital domain which is rife with easy praise as well as loving, smothering, character assassinations.

We need to recognize that we are living now in a time that is stretched, where space is contracted and compressed, where the material blends with the immaterial, and chaos takes the form of order. The world now emerging is of a different (dis)order, and it operates through a dense mental collective field. We are seeing a change in our understanding of phenomenon; the world, and our sense of reality, is mutating and we haven't yet fully upgraded our faculties to correctly interpret this. What we are seeing may be new, yet we are still largely filtering it through the corrupted Wounded Mind. We are losing our sense of *context*. We see the phenomena yet are finding it harder and harder to fully place it in a context of significance. We have altered our means and ways of communication, which inevitably will have significant affects upon our societies. Societies are organisms of communication and information. We are morphing that organism. And at the same time, we are not only carrying the Wounded Mind but also projecting it through countless individual expressions.

Our sense perceptions as human beings are entangled with our social and cultural environments. As they shift, change, and mutate, we shall expect changes too in our organs of perception. Yet if our perceptions are blocked or manipulated then we have a distorted view of the world that then corrupts our mental faculties. If we put these two factors together — a global-technical communications platform and a collective distorted perception — then we have a serious situation that affects all of our futures. We have the capacity for mass communication in our digital world, and yet there is the danger that — like the Tower of Babel — most people are talking in tongues that only they themselves can make any real sense of. Many social movements, memes and trends, begin with a unified spirit of action only to later dissolve into separatist ideals, conflicting opinions, and the rest. In current times we have moved from a vertical Tower of Babel to a horizontal one — a web of wagging tongues where everyone is at the centre and at the periphery at the same time. It excludes almost nothing, stretching out to ever-expanding digital frontiers. It is a realm of signs that is replacing the word; a contact now is deemed a friend; a click becomes a like. As we further engage in a cacophony of online voices the authoritative powers solidify their own position through the disunified and estranged actions of any counter force.

The digital traces of information that we leave behind as we weave through the online realm are taking precedence over our 'real life' and who we actually are. In order to gain access, we must move and pass through an ever-increasing array of algorithms. We may think we are moving unnoticed as part of the ongoing freeway of constant digital traffic; yet we have been monitored and recorded for posterity. And then if we do something to alert the system — we make a false step, post the wrong words, or go in debt, for example — then the system will flag you up and take an interest. We only raise the alarm when we step out of the grooves of the expected social norms, or raise a head above the apathy line.

The Spectral Gaze of Apathy

A crisis has come upon us, seemingly out of nowhere, as if an invader upon a sleeping army. This invader is the Wounded Mind, the psycho-pathogen, and the sleeping army is our collective minds. This invader sweeps over us, treading upon our eyelids and con-torting our dream state. No-one really seems to know what to do, or how to properly wake up. We are groggy still, and maybe slightly dizzy. It's not clear whether we, as people, are able to form our opinions anymore — we have reduced our utterances into daily tweets of abbreviated characters and emoticons. We are deep within our seas of comments and judgements yet shallow with our vision. A growing 'quietism' is creeping into the mass mind. Sometimes there is a sudden flash and we sense a feeling of increasing anonymity and obscurity. In this we feel and recognize our vulnerability — as individuals, as nations, and as a species. And then it is gone as the Wounded Mind comes back to the fore.

The growing crisis is not only one of the flesh — our physical lives, jobs, family and social institutions — but also of the spirit. It renders our psyche disenfranchised, fragmented, and in disarray, as if loose from its moorings. It takes away our interest of engagement, leaving us as sleepy spectators. As early as 1925 the social critic Walter Lippmann wrote that 'the private citizen today has come to feel rather like a deaf spectator in the back row ... that ... cannot quite manage to keep awake.'[3] There is political scepticism and apathy, and great amounts of seething resentment against incumbent political systems the world over. The current debacle over Brexit is just one reminder of the disarray, in-fighting, and manipulation of public opinion on display. Most thinking people have come to realize that the forms of democracy given to us are a sham and that political systems are rigged from the inside out.

Money, power, unseen cabals, criminal networks, offshoring practices, and illicit deals are what make much of the world turn. Individual voting is nothing more than mass appeasement. There are unavoidable systems within systems that constrain, control, and which keep most of us in check within our day to day lives. We are chained to our work obligations, to our debts, and to our consumerist desires that are inflamed and fed by media propaganda. Our educational institutions have taught us the bare minimal; only enough to serve as good workers, and never enough to inspire our visions. And all the while the elite minority in the world are somehow not obligated to these systems. This may have always been the case throughout most of human history. Yet today the visibility of this inequity has never before been so evident.

Governments, in the Western world especially, are façades for a behind-the-scenes monopoly of power that operates with an almost unseen hand. The full-frontal farce of politics, like a show of dancing can-can girls, is propped up by flashy marketing. The real power now lies beyond the nation state and moves beyond the spaces and territories – and borders – that increasingly regulate us. It is a power that attempts to restrict free movement within its spaces by monopolizing the information of anything that moves. Our modern institutional leaders are like false shamanic figures, plying us with their technical trickery, NLP language, and gimmicky propaganda. They aim for our emotional centres and breed fears as well as create great trivializations. They morph complex issues into simple solutions that they sell like snake oil. Welcome to the age of the Great Simplification.

Such leaders act like gurus, gaining fame and notoriety or popularity rather than respect. They have become performers that seek to hypnotize us rather than convince us. We are listening to the new Pied Pipers whose 'magic music' is aimed at the masses. We listen to it on our headphones, trance-like, as we make our daily, debilitating commutes. Those people we used to hold in high public esteem are no longer seen as being worthy. For the most part this involves politicians. Some would argue that public servants are corrupt, entertainers are crass, film stars and footballers are over-paid, and bankers are pigs. And that's about the modern sum of it. And yet so many of us still accept this as the normal run of life. Isn't that crazy?

We are being persuaded by the Wounded Mind to prefer the artificial to the real; to support and invest in disinterested motives that are more harmful than good. Our modern bureaucracies are as antiquated as the sewer systems under London. It is a vaudeville show rather than a real road-map. We angrily take part in demon-strations and rallies, with slogans and placards, not fully realizing how we are just adding to the instruments of the show. Indignation has become an ingredient for the cultural carnival and not the catalyst for real change. Even many radicals are becoming out-of-date as they use worn-out slogans time and time again. The

'modern' way of protest by piling into the streets, chanting, con-
verging on institutional buildings, and handing over petitions no
longer has an effectual place in our societies. The only way that lies
open to us is the way of creation. I have already quoted from
Buckminster Fuller where he urges us not to fight the existing
system. He tells us that if we wish for real change then it is for us to
create a new model that makes the existing reality obsolete. By
fighting against the existing model, we are only adding fuel to the
fire. The Wounded Mind peddles an obsolete perspective, and one
that it is imperative we break out of (as I discuss in Part 3).

We have become embroiled and immersed in a global mental
web of false ideologies and power that most of us are not aware of.
We are the consumers, the audience, the participators, and the
captives of this pervasive spell. It is almost imperceptible, invisible
– seemingly unintentional – and yet it is precisely deliberate, albeit
with built-in unintended consequences. It pervades our physical
and digital spaces and acts as if it is a natural inhabitant, in its
homeland. Who can resist or pull away from a reality that fleetingly
appears as if it is a dreamworld? It does not seemingly promote
itself and yet is promoted by others; it has no name, no theory, no
banners or webpages. And yet everyone supports it by not opposing
it. It becomes a part of us by *giving us its mind*. The Wounded Mind
strives for all of us to share its dull, baroque, power-hungry mind.

There is no longer any credible incumbent model – moral, cultural, or political – that can truly shape the new institutions that the
world needs. It must come from a new inward spirit – from a
human institution, a collective spirit. Contemporary culture and its
attendant social institutions lack soul – that's the bottom line. We
are severely 'lacking greater agents able to transform undercurrent
into culture, trend into movement, individual gesture into universal
meaning.'[4] The individual today is more vulnerable to manipulation than they realize. It is the sea in which they swim and breathe –
as such, it is virtually unnoticeable. We have the delusion that we
are born into a 'blank slate' world, and then upon this we learn to
perceive things as they really are. In fact, the truth is contrary to this.

We are born into a world that is pre-constructed with its cultural and social biases. These then conform the new born mind into accepting the mental programming it is given, through institutional structures, social norms, and cultural ideologies. The result of this is that our cultural conditioning dissuades us from the search for meaning. They persuade us away from such a course by distracting us with false counterparts. Yet as the Persian poet Rumi said, false gold exists because there is real gold. We need to adjust our mode of 'being-in-the-world' — our so-called 'meaningless context' is not incurable, if we can see the ailment. As the aphorism from playwright Bertolt Brecht goes: 'Go search for knowledge, you who are freezing.' We have been conjured into a collective spell that has given us the Wounded Mind. Within this foreign mind — or foreign installation — there lies a constant niggling anxiety.

Social Anxiety

We are anxious about the place we occupy in the world; not only from a material standpoint but from an emotional one. The world is our home, and we need to feel 'at home' in the world. This gives us a natural contradiction and tension between our innate humanity and the madness we see in the world around us. And yet this madness pulls us in because it demands that we comply with its norms and ways if we wish to, as they say, 'get on in the world'. Our modern societies are based around the motif of success without forming any basis of life meaning other than the status of success and the ability to acquire goods. The status of success for the most part merely refers to a social status within our own community and peer group. A major anxiety for many people is the fear of anonymity, of being 'a nobody'. The response to this often comes in the role of attention-seeking, which is a diluted form of seeking acknowledgement and recognition. We use others as mirrors for that which we are seeking. We want to love our self as well as to receive love from the world. And this is our great undertaking as well as our great confusion. What we generally see in the world around us right now is a mess. What we are really seeking through all of our concerns — our longings for money, fame, status, etc — is love and acceptance.

We may say that not much has changed since Tolstoy wrote *The Death of Ivan Ilyich*, a novel where the main character is forced through his impending death to consider his life. He realizes that in living the 'good life' in the eyes of his society he was only catering to the superficialities of convention, of status and wealth; and of self-interest and success over and above his family. In recognizing that an authentic life is one of compassion, sympathy, tenderness and love, Ivan finally sees the light, quite literally. Yet why wait until the dying moment? Because the Wounded Mind will do its utmost to make sure that a person does not get to see the truth before. To do so would undermine its very purpose and would throw a light upon the presence of such an insidious, lurking collective mind. Therefore, the Wounded Mind distracts the attention of the person's inner eye through promoting its own narcissistic tendencies.

A constant uncertainty, insecurity, and world weariness has crept into the modern world. The mainstream media does not help this by constantly showing the negative side of sanctioned news rather than the many positive aspects occurring in the world. The Wounded Mind wishes to focus on this suffering and not on the many examples of uplifting development. This predicament has been mentioned by many psychologists, philosophers and mystics. As G.I. Gurdjieff famously said, 'A man will renounce any pleasures you like but he will not give up his suffering.' And out of this suffering can arise feelings of individual futility and apathy. And the cure, it seems, is gratification through other means; such as pleasure indulgences, addiction, and intoxication. This mix of gratification and addiction is an ideal demonstration of how the psycho-pathogen maintains its power over people. Through our modern societies it propagates freedoms whilst covertly developing dependencies.

We may think we are free, yet we are chained to our possessions, our securities, and our fears. Freedom is an ideal that keeps us comfortably confined, as I shall examine further in the next chapter.

Chapter Nine

Normal Unfreedoms

'Fear is the deadliest assassin; it does not kill, but it keeps you from living.'

Popular Saying

*'Fear has many eyes
And can see things underground.'*

Cervantes, Don Quixote

The Universal Declaration of Human Rights contains thirty articles. Nine of those articles directly state the word 'freedom'. We therefore expect that a range of freedoms are our basic human rights. We consider ourselves as 'free' and independent individuals. Sometimes a president of a large nation even goes as far as referring to the 'Freedom-Loving West' – as opposed to, we must surmise, some 'Non-Freedom-Loving Non-West'. And ever since we turned ourselves into a collection of 'civilized societies', we've been trying our hardest to eliminate those uncertain and unknown fears. We always felt relief when we finally knew where our fears were coming from, and we could confront them. Usually they turned out to be not so scary (vampire-like) than we had thought or imagined them to be. When we could see, and perhaps touch them, the darkness surrounding the fear would disappear. Sometimes we would get an 'aha' feeling, and we'd let out a huge sigh. That would make things better. Because when we can see something, we are better placed to do something about it. And we also know just exactly what our capacities and limitations are in such circumstances. Fear, and potential dangers, used to be a lot more familiar to us; but that was when the world was smaller, and our neighbourhoods were a place of home and belonging.

The shift into modernity was considered as a move into a world where calamity and catastrophic disasters would be put to rest. It would be a time where fanciful illusions and ungrounded worries would be washed away. It would be a 'modern' time of certainty and solid progress. It appears that what was once seen as a straight road ahead has turned into a long, winding detour; and the only maps we have are satnavs with annoying actors' voices. Our modern world has done little to extinguish the presence of existential threats – in fact, if anything, they have increased. We no longer have only natural disasters to worry us, we also have the bank/stock markets' crash; corporate collapse; the failure of power grids; jets falling out of skies; children with handguns mowing down other kids at school; or jihadists at pop concerts. It's now a cornucopia of possible death on nearly every street corner, and quite literally in our schools, in our homes, and very definitely in our own heads. As Craig Brown notes, with a touch of parody: 'Every day, there were new Global Warnings about killer viruses, killer waves, killer drugs, killer icebergs, killer meat, killer vaccines, killer killers and other possible causes of imminent death.'[1]

The Wounded Mind spreads its traumatic virus through permeating a fear psychosis within our daily lives. It doesn't necessarily have to be a big 'oh my dear g-d' type of fear. The constant and underlying 'civilized fears' also sustain a persistent nervous energy and anxiety within our collective being. Such modern fears seem to have an almost civilized agenda, where they attempt to make life with fear liveable. This is what Thomas Mathiesen refers to as a 'silent silencing' in that 'it is a part of our everyday life; it is unbounded and is therefore engraved upon us; it is noiseless and therefore passes by unnoticed; and it is dynamic in the sense that in our society it spreads and becomes continually more encompassing.'[2]

We've always considered risks as calculable dangers, where we at least have some capacity to estimate their potential. But fears are now that which we can neither predict nor fully escape from because they flirt too close to our dark fantasies. Whereas risks can be seen as *explosions*, emanating from without, our fears are the *implosions* that erupt from within. The trauma of the Wounded Mind – the *wetiko* psychosis – perpetuates this struggle between a sense of self and some 'other' external, almost alien, agency. This is similar to what don Juan referred to as the *foreign installation*. The German psychoanalyst Erich Fromm wrote that the battlefield for freedom is both within the self and with our institutions. Our dependency, he suggested, begins with the helplessness of being born and needing extra-long dependency and protection. Our human biological weakness, he says, is the very condition of human culture. The result is that there remains a lifelong struggle between the individual self and those overwhelmingly strong powers external to us — or unnatural to us. Fromm noted that we succumb to powers outside of ourselves through being blinded to our inner restraints, compulsions, and fears, which undermine our real power. Fromm made an interesting observation in that the human being, 'is not really the master any more of the world he has built; on the contrary, this man-made world has become his master, before whom he bows down, whom he tries to placate or to manipulate as best he can.'3

The *wetiko* psychosis has turned fear into its own commodity marketplace, and like any good marketplace it requires consumers. And consumers are better at consuming if they are given a valid need. This logic tells us then that fear is planted in as many of us as possible in order to have a need to safeguard against it. It's somewhat akin to saying that so many people are diet-obsessed because our media tells us how important it is to be thin. French sociologist Hugues Lagrange, in his study of fear, came to term as 'derivative fear' that which guides much of our modern behaviour. It acts as a secondary type of fear when there isn't any immediate threat present. It is a sediment, a residue, that outlives any *actual* threat; somehow the shadow of the menace lingers on, haunting us. It shapes our behaviour, regardless of whether any direct threat to us exists. It is this type of fear, I suggest, that is endemic to the Wounded Mind and is seeded into us through our media and social institutions.

This haunting, lingering type of fear is more intangible, invisible, and hence cannot be quantified or reasonably assessed by us. It is, in all ways and forms, a lurking type of fear — slithery, shadowy, and sneaky. It is distasteful, and yet has great power to invade and infect our conscious and unconscious minds. It makes us more susceptible and vulnerable to feelings of insecurity and dis-empowerment. We are open to attack at any time; we are instilled with a lack of trust. And, importantly, we are more willing to obey (i.e., willing obedience) to those authoritative powers that promise defence and security. Any person who has internalized the sense emotions of derivative fear will be more willing to respond to threat, even in the absence of a genuine threat. Such behaviour is self-propelled and is exactly what the collective psychosis wants.

Those of us in so-called 'developed' territories live in some of the most secured societies, pampered with our goods and lifestyles, and yet we feel the most threatened, insecure, vulnerable, and liable to panic than most other societies. The philosopher Richard Rorty notes that we are in danger of winding up into only two types of international social groups: 'the super-rich and the intellectuals, that is, the people who attend international conferences devoted to measuring the harms being done by their super-rich fellow cos-mopolitans.'[4] I would be tempted to add two more international groups – the criminals (drug and people traffickers, the terrorists); and the poor migrants forced to flee from war zones or natural disasters. Rorty goes on to say that if the masses 'can be distracted from their own despair by media-created pseudo-events, including the occasional brief and bloody war, the super-rich will have little to fear.'[5] And so the psychosis shows its full *wetiko* credentials by creating social and class divisions which instil their own fears and struggles.

Psychologically we fear being weak. We despise being seen as downtrodden; as being the 'weakest link' in our family or com-munity. And yet our entertainment media plays on this. The 'weakest' is voted off on Reality TV shows, from the coward in the jungle to the geek in the Big Brother house. The 'weakest link' is eliminated in the pseudo-quiz show of the same name. These morals teach us that being weak means exclusion, exile, being outcast – the evicted person from Big Brother walks out to a barrage of boos. There is nothing quite so caustic as public humiliation. We no longer need our town square stocks and our rotting vegetables to throw – we have mainstream and social media to add further public insult to injury. And all this is trauma-food for the collective Wounded Mind. Can we not see that we play it out in front of us – or rather perhaps, *it is being played out for us*? The shadows dance upon the wall of Plato's cave, and we sit entranced and in fear of our weaknesses.

So many things that are presented to us in modern life are little more than transient distractions – the retro fad or fashion; the one-hit wonder pop star that was a reality TV cast-off; the TV jingle you sing in the shower; the over-hyped diet; the latest juice recipe; etc. And yet the intangible, lurking fear remains, shadowy and ever-present. And this type of fear not only seeps deep down into us, it also reminds us that our real fear is being incapable of escaping our own condition of being afraid. In many cases, this lingering internal fear has forced us to give permission for external actors to intervene in our private lives. We are fear-driven to give away our power to others, which is exactly what the Wounded Mind wants – a collective power to traumatize us. As film-maker Adam Curtis said: 'In an age when all the grand ideas have lost credibility, fear of a phantom enemy is all the politicians have left to maintain their power.'[6]

We are offered our 'new securities' in the form of unfreedoms. In other words, we have opened the door and allowed the wolf to enter as a guest.

Privacy, Unfreedoms & (In)Securities

Article 12 of the Universal Declaration of Human Rights states 'Freedom from Interference with Privacy, Family, Home and Correspondence'. Yet now the concept and ideas around privacy are rapidly shifting. The idea of privacy has undergone a modern upheaval, and it has now colonized the public realm. Privacy has become the domain of our confessional societies, where it is now divorced from secrecy – it is no longer an intimate space. It was once a much more guarded and secure place; a place where personal traumas were veiled. Yet today it has undergone an almost irreversible swing with the rise of the public sphere. The privacy domain and the public sphere are now collaborators as part of the modern pseudo-transparent society. The internal and individual Wounded Mind of old has been transformed into a collective and public confessional.

We lived for centuries with the medieval sense of confession; i.e., an intimate, confidential whisper to the priest or through the tortured confession ripped out of us in hidden retreats. Now we are treated to public confessions bordering on self-advertising, from the blogs, social media posts, to videos that display an exhibitionism once frowned on by most cultures. Secrecy – the secret self – is now seen as something anti-social. This behaviour and attitude is part of the collective psychosis that wishes to share, spread, and influence others into joining this public, pseudo-cathartic process. Our technologies that allow such public confessionals merely reflect our human condition; they show externally that which we normally keep hidden. Physical, social and psychical exposure is now a part of the general collective mind. And what is more, this modern mode of the Wounded Mind has attempted to impose a manageable control over unruly social chaos and uncertainties.

A rational mindset was brought to bear, according to sociologist Zygmunt Bauman, 'to bring the world of humans, hitherto vexingly opaque, bafflingly unpredictable and infuriatingly disobedient and oblivious to human wishes and objectives, into order: a *complete, incontestable* and *unchallenged order*. Order under the indomitable rule of Reason.'[7]* This 'unchallenged order' needs an obedient collective mindset, and the Wounded Mind – complete with its traumas – is the ideal material with which to manage this. Despite the overall global coherence and forms of political, financial, and trading collaborations, today's so-called modern cultures are increasingly internally fragmented. Our domestic norms have dissolved; we can no longer identify with the old symbols and values that once gave us meaning. The original coherence found within

---

*Italics in original.

indigenous cultures has been systematically targeted and eradicated over centuries. Modern life has eliminated our ancient, pagan connections and re-assembled them into contemporary forms of regulated control and obedience. We have entered a period of increased uncertainty in terms of the human condition. This has contributed to our collective traumas which are being amplified publicly through what I have been calling, throughout this book, the Wounded Mind.

Today, people can boast that they have managed to make hundreds of new friends in a day on Facebook, whereas previously it would have taken us more than one lifetime to accomplish such a feat. Yet we loosely use the term 'friend' to describe superficial acquaintance. Professor Robin Dunbar, an evolutionary anthropologist, tells us that most of us can only maintain around 150 meaningful relationships; an amount imposed by our evolutionary upbringing (now called the 'Dunbar number'). It related to the number of humans who could come together as cultural groups in efficient cooperation – perhaps even an ancestral survival strategy. Such groupings, and cultural friendships, provided us certain meaning and known constants. Modern life has given us the global network to replace a close-knit social community of friendships. As a result, our rooted meanings have been unmoored from the community harbour. Dunbar noted, 'you can "friend" 500, 1,000, even 5,000 people with your Facebook page, but all save the core 150 are mere voyeurs looking into your daily life.'[8] The desire to find friends is at the heart of our social being; now the context has shifted into a need for self-fulfilment and a sense of self-assurance. In other words, to seek acknowledgement from others. As we continue to lose our sense of local community, it will be natural that people turn more and more to the collective Wounded Mind as a form of security and stability.

The need for security, which is being rolled out as a social stabilizing force, is yet another form of power. And it has been the same throughout most of human history – we give our cooperation to be ruled, and this is welcomed by the rulers. In fact, it is expected by them, and they rely upon it. It is this compliant agreement that sustains authority: visible enforcement then slips into new social norms and 'expected' behaviour. It also works through seduction by the arousal of our desires and the supply of our satisfactions. Social management (a.k.a. security) is a mixture of glossy public relations and our own complicit self-surveillance through the smartphone, the health tracker, the smart watch, etc. To find meaning, it seems, we must also provide data. As philosopher Jean-Pierre Dupuy observes, 'We are condemned to perpetual vigilance.'[9]

To all intents and purposes, modern life has become dependent upon surveillance – and it is also an addictive dependency. Once we have it, we feel it is not enough and we need more, until we come to the point where we realize we cannot do without it because we have created our own psychological state of feeling afraid. Quite simply, fear breeds fear. Insecurities are now becoming the norm of today's increasingly securitized societies. Insecurity has insinuated itself into our social and political configurations. That is, in/security is now systemic; but it is far from static. Earlier dystopic visions of in/security, notably from George Orwell (*Nineteen Eighty-Four*) and Aldous Huxley (*Brave New World*), regarded such cultures as being more solidified. Security and power/control regimes were in place, fiercely positioned and intimidating. Or, in Huxley's case, they were engrained within our compelling pleasures. Today, our in/securities and regimes of power/control are fluid, uncertain, non-visible, and constantly on the move; they adapt, re-position, and re-configure themselves.

Fear and insecurity are now diffused and nonlinearly scattered throughout our diverse cultures. They are unpredictable, unclear, unanchored, and with no direct agenda or cause. We are haunted by a continually propagandized realm of unknowns, by a threatening menace that we are told is everywhere within a thousand faces. These intangible 'floating' threats are often cleverly packaged by our societal propaganda agencies into 'knowns', such as named terrorist organizations, or stereotyped into ethnic groups. In other words, the 'usual suspects' are rolled out, each time with a different name or toy-like acronym. In return, 'we the people' often define ourselves against such threats as a way of being seen as apart from them: 'We all need to mark the enemies of security in order to *avoid being counted among them*... We need to accuse in order to be absolved; to exclude in order to avoid exclusion.'[10] And this has become the public face of our collective Wounded Mind. *It fears* – and thus we must fear.

In the end, such 'security' actually generates increased insecurity, either as a by-product or perhaps as a deliberate in-built policy. This has created a 'security obsession', whereby ordinary citizens are encouraged to respond to new insecurities by two ways. These are either a strategy of defence (e.g., stockpiling supplies), or by attack (such as supporting extreme government measures, including increased domestic surveillance). Our public-collective mindset is further conditioned with feelings of insecurity, often encouraged by political rhetoric, and sustained by urban fortification, techno-logical surveillance, and economic vulnerability. Our modern dense urban enclaves are now filling up with gated communities, privately-patrolled neighbourhoods, and security zones. We are more and more living alongside visible and invisible walls, barri-cades, watchtowers and enclosures – all aggressively guarded by a burgeoning force of armed security. The Wounded Mind wishes to make us all feel vulnerable and wounded in some way.

Despite all this we need to constantly remind ourselves that this Wounded Mind needs *our minds* through which to manifest. It needs our willing compliance, and in this lies the clever yet das-tardly manoeuvre of presenting the inhuman – and the inhumane – as something normal.

Normalizing the Inhuman as Human

Adolf Eichmann was put on trial in Jerusalem charged with involvement in the death of about six million humans. His defence tried to convince the court that his only motive was the *job well done*. That is, to do the best he could for his superiors, as he would any job. He had no personal interest or grudges against the people and could not stomach the sight of murder. He was merely acting out his orders, providing loyal service to his superiors, and the death of millions was its collateral damage. Let us think on this for a moment – is there nothing wrong in wanting to fulfil orders to the best of one's ability? Here we have only to refer to the infamous Stanley Milgram experiments to realize that we might well do almost anything if a person in a white coat tells us to do so.[*] We have been quite thoroughly socially conditioned to accept and submit to various displays of power.

As I discussed in a previous book, what I refer to as the 'Modernity Project' has inserted within the collective psyche a subconscious obedience to authority, as a form of artificial conditioning.[†] Within complex societies the threat of chaos, and thus the loss of social privileges, is usually enough to gain support for constraining security measures. Yet to achieve this there has been a subtle and ingenious – yet devastating – manoeuvre to acclimatize and desensitize people to acts of inhumanity. As Jack Forbes pointed out, the *wetikos* are not only the brutes or those people who hold great power, they are also 'the nice people in the offices, the typists, the lab technicians, the clerks and, of course, the owners, directors, stockholders, senators, generals and presidents who use, profit from, and feed on human exploitation.'[11]

It is a Kafkaesque scenario where bureaucracy and its workmanlike rationale cancels out all notions of soul, meaning, compassion, and especially love. Notions of 'being' and 'meaning' are dissected and compartmentalized into the concept of the loyal servant. And in this regard, those agencies of external authority – including also the Wounded Mind – have won over the individual human spirit. Erich Fromm, in his highly regarded work *The Fear of Freedom*, recognized that a hugely influential, almost secret, power was being exercised over the whole of society in a way that has prejudiced our social mindset. In this regard he wrote that – 'Because we have freed ourselves of the older overt forms of

---

[*] See Milgram, S. *Obedience to Authority: An Experimental View*. New York: HarperCollins, 1974.

[†] See my book *The Struggle for your Mind*.

authority, we do not see that we have become the prey of a new kind of authority. We have become automatons who live under the illusion of being self-willing individuals.'[12] And it is this illusion, I argue, that is being sustained and developed by the traumatized Wounded Mind. The result is that we have entered into a collective psychological crisis.

This contemporary crisis – our current psychosis – is that many of us are, in the words of Fromm, living under the illusion of being self-willing individuals. The ingenious manoeuvre of the Wounded Mind has given us the illusion – or delusion – that everything we think and therefore do, originates from our own will. The frustrating contradiction here is that we can, and do, have individual agency – if we can act from *our own minds*. To achieve this, we must separate our sense of *genuine self* from the programmed *social self* that acts as our personality – our mask. We need to 'wake up' and see the way in which our lives have been, and continue to be, manipulated and programmed. I speak more on the manifestation of the *genuine self* in the next section.

At present, we occupy a space where anything might happen, yet nothing can be known with any certainty. Whilst we are concerned and focused upon the future, we also experiment, invent, and share a vague collective image of the world. We prefer not to admit to ourselves that we have no clear idea of what lays ahead, for this is uncomfortable and unsettling. Yet the future has to be in our hands; the only real and genuine future must be through exorcising fear from within us – to cut out its roots (to root it out) and to expel it from our collective mind and heart.

For now, many of us are still very much living within a collective dream. It is a dream of spectacle, carnival, abstraction, distraction, overload, and the intangible. Subconsciously, we fear slipping into inauthenticity and an inner void. Yet it's time to wake up. It is time to gain a gnostic vision. It is time to acknowledge our wounds in order to find our healing. It is time to turn to the genuine self. As the indigenous people of Bioko like to say – 'Let us get nearer to the fire, so that we can see what we are saying.' The fire begins in Part Three.

Part Three

THE SEARCH FOR THE SELF

Part Three discusses how we may break free from this psychosis by embarking on a gnostic quest for connecting with a transcendental source in our lives. In these final chapters, I talk about how to embark on a personal path and a quest for the genuine self. I discuss how it is imperative we reach for an understanding of what it means to be human so that we may find our soulful freedom.

Chapter Ten

The Gnostic Vision

'We must discover our illusions before we can even realize that we have been sleepwalking.'

Daniel Boorstin

'Is this life real
that I am living –
Is this life real?
Spirits everywhere
Tell me!
Is this life real?'

Jack Forbes

At the end of Part One of this book I talked about how our modern age has seemingly neglected the inner world of the human being. I referred to this as being the metaphysical malaise. I further discussed how this contributed to many people feeling powerless in the face of external forces, and gave a critique of our modern times in Part Two. In short, I suggested that we have been sold a lie; that we have been conditioned to conform rather than to express our innate creativity, imagination, and wonder. We have been taught to accept the buffering of social forces and to adapt to them passively, as would a leaf in the wind. Such a conditioned view of the world and of the self leads to a self-fulfilling prophecy. This self-fulfilling prophecy may support those systems attached to the Wounded Mind, yet they do nothing for the genuine human self.

If a person believes that they can only exert a paltry degree of influence over their life, then this is what they will encounter, and the events that they experience may indeed seem to be random and chaotic. If a person views their life as being arranged by circumstances beyond their control, then this will follow them for the rest of their days. It is almost the same as believing that we exist on the back of a dead rock hurtling through lifeless space. The myth we choose for ourselves is the myth that will guide us. If we succumb to the dominant falsehood of the Wounded Mind, then we shall be steered by our compliance to this fiction. Our personal failures in life often result not from poor intentions or the absence of intention, but from the inability to see and implement our genuine aspirations. That is, our personal gnosis is often shrouded to us. This is the secret of the veil imposed upon us by the mental pathogen.

Sometimes, however, we are subject to more than just social forces. There are times when life across the whole planet seems irritable and on edge. We must realize that none of us, the animal and vegetable kingdom included, live in a vacuum. Sometimes the wrong wind blows, as they say. Take the Levant, which is an easterly wind that blows in the western Mediterranean Sea and through the Strait of Gibraltar. For the past several years I have lived in Andalusia and the *Levante*, as the Spanish call it, blows often a dry, hot wind that soon begins to make the locals irritable. There's just something in the energy of the wind. The same thing can be said for winds across the planet. Perhaps the same can be said for solar winds; after all, these are already known to cause electromagnetic disruption. What I am saying is that there are also natural external impacts that make us feel restless and put us in a state of tension. Many ancient traditions knew about this. As philosopher J.G. Bennett writes:

> In a more subtle and pervasive manner, great regions of the earth's surface, and sometimes even the whole of the earth, become subject to a state of tension that produces in people a strong sense of dissatisfaction with their conditions of life. They become irritable or aggressive, apprehensive, nervous and highly suggestible.[1]

Bennett goes on to say that people unconsciously project outwards this state of inner tension, and become hostile and angry with people and with the world in general.

Without any inner filters of our own we are defenceless against such mass psychoses. Such psychoses can be temporary – such as in war or revolution – or can be more lasting, as in our mental conditioning. As a child, I was told what we call an 'old wives' tale' by my parents. They told me not to pull an ugly face because the wind might change while I did so. And if the wind changed, then I would be stuck with that ugly face forever. In a similar manner, if we pull an 'ugly mindset' and the proverbial wind changes, then we'll be stuck in that psychic state for our lives. A study of human history will show us that many cultures, nations, and empires have carried a particular psychological state over long periods of time. Without knowledge of how our internal psyches are impacted, and how our inner tensions and dissatisfactions can be created, we have no conscious defence or awareness of them. The result is often that we end up projecting these tensions externally, validating and amplifying the Wounded Mind through our relations and behaviour.

Continuing external tensions and dissatisfactions creates conditions for further external conflict, conquest, and control. These then also irritate the inner state of the human, and without adequate psychic defences or filters they can cause internal tensions to rise, adding to the endless cycle of external-internal tensions. Often that which we see happening in the world is a reflection of our individual and collective inner states. It is common for us to project our dissatisfactions outwards, finding fault in others, or criticizing our job, our work colleagues, our useless technologies, and anything else that comes across our radar. This state can also lead to increased self-absorption, self-importance, and self-pity. We must be aware of this and aim to break the vicious cycle.

As I explained in Part One, there are deliberate social conditions — such as compulsory education — which arrests the development of inner faculties of discernment in favour of producing 'efficient workers'. As a collective, we lack the discrimination to understand the interplay between external and internal forces. Because of this, the general 'public mind' — that is largely moulded from social-cultural forces — coalesces into the Wounded Mind, that also infects the collective unconscious. Under these conditions it becomes more difficult to raise humankind to a higher level of awareness, perception, and understanding. And yet this is what is required. Again, quoting Bennett:

> If a new world is to come, we must first create it in ourselves. You
> may ask how the work of a few people can change the world. It has
> always been so. Ideas are powerful, not organizations. Nothing can
> be done by outward force; everything can be done by inner strength.[2]

To have inner strength requires that we carry vision within us. The
gnostic vision is one such path to this awareness.

The Gnostic Vision

Gnosticism is an expression of a particular knowledge of reality. It
is a knowledge of direct awareness that transforms the human
psyche and heightens the perceptual faculties. In its essence, it is
spiritual knowledge arrived at intuitively. A genuine Gnostic path is
not a religious one. If anything, it can be said to be an inner chain of
transmission. This transmission – or, intuitive knowledge – provides information about the structure of reality, yet it does not
provide any ready-made 'truths'. Instead, it provides the means
whereby a person may approach the 'truth' of reality themselves. It
is not a system but rather exists as a systematic body of knowledge.
And this chain of transmission has existed at all times and continues to exist in contemporary cultures today. Gnosis is a specific
perception vis-à-vis Reality. It provides a person (the 'knower') with
direct experience that is beyond all forms of secondary perception
or cultural systems of knowledge.

What this body of intuitive knowledge says is that the human
being is not purely a material creature – a physical complex made
up of thoughts and emotions – but is a vehicle for an indwelling
spirit. And contact with this inner spirit brings awareness beyond
the normal range of perceptions. The Gnostic path aims at the
awakening of this spiritual impulse within humanity and the individual. This spiritual component is the source of our inner revelations, our visions, and our dreams – our longing for completeness.
The spiritual component is in active communication with our inner
self and often attempts to communicate through symbols, dreams,
synchronicities, and non-verbal means. Yet it requires an active
participation from the person in order to develop beyond these

communicative transmissions. The symbols given out by the spiritual component can reveal a path of inner psychological development towards gnosis. Gnostic teachings state that our soul is the result of a prior descent, and that we have a future destiny for return. Within us resides a residual memory of wholeness. It is this residual memory that we may feel as a 'nagging' or 'urging' from deep within us, as though we have forgotten something, or we need to accomplish some task. This task is to seek and nurture our own inner development. It is this which exists as the antidote to the mass mental pathogen that afflicts us as human beings.

However, such inner psychological development is not an easy task, for we are surrounded, and often penetrated, by forces that seek to dominate our vulnerable state. They compel us with foolish thoughts and behaviour. We are imbued with unconscious compulsions that act against our developmental potential. These forces have been given many names over the years, as we have seen in Part One of this book. It is our duty, as human beings, to overcome these negative forces. Otherwise, we shall remain under their dominant sway. As we have seen, this renders us in a form of psychic slavery. These forms of psychic dominance can also be regarded as *aspects of evil*, in that they are in conflict (dualism) with our need for inner growth. The acknowledgement of these dualisms in material life is also a part of the Gnostic vision.

Gnosis as a path of wisdom takes evil (also considered as *error* or *deviance*) seriously in that it recognizes that there exist forces of 'psychic dominance'. This recognition is especially important for our contemporary world, for such forces are not only highly active now but they are also more visible in their machinations. Yet knowing evil is not the same as doing evil. The modern Gnostic vision sees these degenerative impulses at work. The sense of the 'alien mind', or the alienation of consciousness, must be felt and experienced before it can be recognized for what it is. The Wounded Mind must be known and named. Only then can true awareness be activated. This process toward self-development requires that the 'shadow side' be seen and its existence acknowledged. As the psychologist C.G. Jung wrote – '[beneath the] thin veneer of culture the wild beast lurks . . . But the beast is not tamed by locking it up in a cage. *There is no morality without freedom.*'[3] The Gnostic path does not regard this recognition of deviance as deep pessimism, but rather as necessary and a functional insight toward knowing freedom.

Those persons who choose to ignore the existence of these 'shadow forces' may turn to self-deception as an antidote. Yet this condition cannot relieve the soul of its knowing. It is only a mode of evasion that seeks refuge in transitory diversions and distractions. This is one reason why our modern cultures are so 'diversion heavy', with their entertainments and consumer goodies. The bottom line is that the inner spiritual development of the human is an undeniable reality. There may be those people who like to tell themselves, and others, that such 'inner growth' is a fantasy — yet it is these people who perpetuate the fantasy within themselves. The reality of the situation cannot be denied, only ignored. Human life is, to use Gnostic words, a process of soul-making. The spiritual impulse seeks release and in the earthly realm this must be achieved through a vessel, a vehicle. This is the human condition. Truth is not a relative position — only human truths are.

Those who prefer to identify wholly with the physical-material world to the exclusion of their spiritual essence can be said, in Gnostic terms, to be spiritually dead. Perhaps this is one reason why our current entertainments are filled with movies, TV series, and books about zombies and the walking dead. We are staring ourselves in the face and we haven't yet realized it. The joke is an open secret, yet closed to most people. There is also much talk in wisdom traditions about death, dying, and journeys into the underworld. The dead must learn to come alive in life or they remain forever in a reality that is Hades. The Gnostic vision recognizes the dark as well as the light. It sees both in operation, and not necessarily in opposition. The polarities must be faced, balanced out, and not ignored. The shadows must be seen and identified, for it is through the darkness where the light comes in. Similarly, no healthy tree can disown its own roots, that grow deep into the dark soil below. To do so would bring death. We are rooted in our own soils, too. According to mythologist Joseph Campbell: 'It is not society that is to guide and save the creative hero, but precisely the reverse. And so every one of us shares the supreme ordeal ... not in the bright moments of his tribes' great victories, but in the silences of his personal despair.'[4]

Although this might sound a little dramatic, we should note that this is a symbolic-mythical rendering. What this does tell us is that we first need to face the uncomfortable truths of our predicament before we can take the first step forward. Or, as Paul Brunton put it – 'Humanity swims forward on a stream formed from its own tears.'[5] The Gnostic vision tells us that so many of us are preoccupied with the external circumstances of our lives to the extent that we neglect, or do not even sense, this higher longing. The world of dualisms is a necessary one, for through this struggle we are able to see genuine truths as opposed to relative ones. And yet it is not an easy path to choose:

> The sturdy struggle of reason against passion, intuition against suggestion, truth against self-interest, individuality against the mass and contemplation against convention is an unending one. But it is also an honourable one ... It is both a blunder and a sin to take the easier path.[6]

The external events of the mental pathogen – the Wounded Mind or *wetiko* virus – are in a sense necessary in order to compel us towards the crucial inner event: the awakening of our spiritual essence. The Gnostic vision recognizes this conflict between external delusions and inner development. We can say that we are struggling with our collective unconscious, and this struggle is bringing to the surface all the evils in the human character. All our ugliest and unpleasant passions and desires are finding release. The horrors and violence that have characterized so much of our so-called 'modern lives' are the manifestations of the grand human struggle to recognize, identify, and finally break free from the collective psychosis. All this washing of 'dirty laundry' in public is part of the process needed in the healing of the Wounded Mind.

We can compare this with the mystical 'Dark Night of the Soul', the purging of the soul on its ascent towards the unknowable Source. We could say that our lives are like one long, ongoing attempt to resist the unknown. We live in the present, and yet we often attempt to resist it. We need to open our eyes and to be sensitive and aware to each moment, to recognize each moment as unique and new, and to be receptive to this. We also need to recognize the evil that is flowing around us for what it is. As I have mentioned several times, we can only *see* a thing if we first identify it for what it is. The Wounded Mind also represents all the emanations that we, as a collective species, have emitted from within us. It is a vicious circle whereby we both receive and transmit, and we are caught in its dark web. Collectively we are needing to purge the ugly aspects of our unconscious from us. Yet to be mentally and emotionally unharmed in this process we also need to observe what is happening and to take a step back. Once we recognize a thing for what it is, it loses its power and dominion over us. The Gnostic vision is about having this perception and inner intuition and recognition. Not having this inner vision may lead us to fear the things that lurk out there in our lives. As the sailors of old used to say about the unknown, uncharted waters – *There Be Dragons*. Such dragons entrap us psychologically, making escape no longer a physical question but a mental and emotional one.

Things in the world may seem to be in a bad state – yet the light is coming through. First it will appear in the anomalies which are hidden from us by dominant mainstream forces under the sway of the Wounded Mind. These anomalies, however, are coming in. And they are here to break with the old dominant forces. I have discussed these dark forces in Part One and Part Two of this book. Now, in Part Three, I will discuss the personal paths we each can take in order to reach further toward our own transcendental connection. The Gnostic path is open to each person, each heart, as long as it genuinely reaches out for the healing. And we each begin with our individual quest for the self.

Chapter Eleven

The Quest for the Self

'I do not have to justify my quest for spirituality in physical terms. If you ask me to do so, it means that you understand nothing of spirituality.'

Henryk Skolimowski

'Tohsa sasa Nikon 'hren'

(Trans. 'Do not let your mind fall')
Mohawk Iroquois saying

The powers and capabilities within the human psyche are far beyond what we have been taught. We have a vast range of powerful potential within — yet for such a long time these capacities have been slumbering under a veil. We have at our disposal vast reservoirs of imagination and intention. Taken together, these can assist us on our quest for self. Whoever does not come to recognize the necessity for such a quest through an inner need of their own, may one day be brought to it out of the need of self-defence in the face of the everyday struggles of life. For the rest of us, that day has arrived in this moment. Once the need to seek for something within ourselves becomes a conscious choice, we have entered upon the Quest.

Entering the Quest

Something is not quite right ... you *feel* it ... you may have experienced this feeling, this nagging, for a long time. So, you most probably just try to ignore it and hope that it goes away; but sooner or later the persistent nagging finally brings an idea to your mind — there's something very odd about the way the world is. Maybe you feel like you are at the cinema watching a film, and yet you sense there must be something wrong about the film you are seeing. The images are all there, but

Contd

> there's a feeling that something is out of sequence, or the frames are running out of 'normal' time. However, after a while you get used to the style of the film, and your senses adjust to its rhythm and you lose the sense of strangeness, and you get pulled into the show and you go along with the ride...
>
> ... The film tells you that the world has no grand meaning, that human life is an accidental anomaly – but as you walk down the street, engage with friends, fall in love, follow your dreams, you experience meaning and significance... But wait, there's that glitch in the film again – something about its 'randomness' and 'meaninglessness' doesn't make *sense* ... your personal experience has shown you something different ... and then there's that nagging feeling again ... somewhere – wasn't there?

Life is something that people go through with trial, joy, adventure, challenge, love, and all the rest. This is the same for all of us, yet it doesn't always take place on the same playing field. There is a different perspective we can take – a different *position* vis-à-vis the world. We can see the world in which we live as solely an exterior phenomenon; or we can choose to view it also as an expression of our interior life. Perception is everything. And whoever controls or has influence over this perception, rules the roost.

For me personally, the cosmos is not just the expression of mathematical equations, but is the play of lyrical forces that, like a living being, is intoxicated with love and wonder, and the joyful curiosity of adventure. I sometimes wonder what it would be like to live with the view that human life is the result of random, accidental forces; as a meaningless happening that forces us to live out our years as part of an arbitrary universe. I am reminded of the 'Myth of Sisyphus', a figure of Greek mythology who was condemned to repeat for eternity the same meaningless task of pushing a boulder up a mountain, only to see it roll down again – and then to push it up again, ad infinitum. This lifeless exterior view of life is for me somewhat absurd.[*] Yet the

---

[*] No wonder then that the existentialist French philosopher Albert Camus wrote an essay titled, 'The Myth of Sisyphus' (1942) describing man's useless search for meaning in an unintelligible world.

physical demands of a normal life compel us to focus our gaze continually on the external, where our daily waking consciousness must deal with all the impacts and noise coming from the outside. It is as if the mental pathogen is trying its hardest to divert us away from interior self-reflection. Yet there is another gaze that peers out onto the world – a gaze from within. It comes from that place where we can deeply feel, intuitively, that there is another perspective upon life; one that is far richer, pervasive, and subtle. Yet it is a perception that does not come freely but must be sought with effort.

For many of us, concerned with everyday survival necessities, there is little time to seek within or to follow a subtle inner urge. Some may seldom, or never, stop to ask themselves 'why am I here?', or 'how did I get here?' This is a fundamental question that appears to bother few people. It is okay to recognize this. Not everyone will be drawn to these questions or issues. Maybe it is not their time. Such a book as this will appeal to the minority. For the rest, there is no Wounded Mind, no collective mental pathogen. There is just a senseless world, seemingly going crazily-wrong right now. And that's just the way it is – get on with it. And then there will be others who will feel, will *sense*, differently. Perhaps that is why you are reading this book right now.

There are those people who only know themselves by the name they wear through life. If pushed, they would find it difficult to truly distinguish themselves from others who bear similar conditioned attitudes and opinions. And yet this realization is hidden so well in material life. Perhaps the shock of such recognition would greatly disturb their mental and emotional balance. And so, many people continue to identify and individualize themselves through the given name they bear, or the job they have elected to perform. This is evident on the occasion when someone is asked *who they are*, they reply either with their name or their occupation. It's a most unsettling question, and for many people they can only answer this by their work function or their given name. It's also true that most of the time this socially accepted question is only asked and directed to a person on the most superficial and banal level; *who* a person actually is remains a lifelong mystery. And this is a condition common to most of us. This is also part of the psychosis that pervades the collective human mind. We have yet to awaken to it.

> ...There's that film again, and it's telling you that your conscious experience is just a consequence of chemical brain functioning — *I do this, I do that, I see this, I feel that, I think this* — ... but the 'I' is just a state of awareness that comes as a by-product from a complex of neurons... But wait a minute — haven't I just been observing my own thoughts and feelings ... standing back from the 'I'? Is this, then, the *real* me? Or is this observer of my thoughts just another neuronal by-product observing the workings of another random by-product? ... Ah, here's the film again, the glitch is gone...

It's also the case that many people rebel against their essential nature, whether they know it or not. People may say a thousand things — or only one thing — and yet in each spoken moment they move away from the essential. Again, what is it to *know oneself*? To grow, to develop, to attain understanding and self-awareness — what do these things mean to the average person? At best, our societies have rendered them as abstract concepts, or as wishful thinking. Within our specific cultures, we have been conditioned to spend very little time and attention upon considering the interior world. As we saw in the chapter on compulsory schooling, we are trained to be compliant, pragmatic, and to function within a factory-like world that is absent of a rich inner life. In fact, the notion of an interior world remains as a luxury for the few. The rest of us have to get on with managing and coping with our 'normal lives'.

And so, we live with many unrecognized questions, failing to notice them from their slumber within us. Do we ever wonder why events have turned out this way? The oddities of our world have gradually become normalized to the point where we cease to see them for what they are — the remnants of a corrupted mind in need of healing. Perhaps we find no compelling need to want to see things in a different way. In fact, some people actively seek to forget. The compulsion to forget is likely to be rationalized by calling it by another name.

Greek mythology tells of how, before the human soul incarnates into this world, it drinks from Lethe, the river of Forgetfulness – one of the five rivers of the underworld – so that it cannot remember its divine origins. Similarly, there is a Jewish legend that speaks of how we are struck on the mouth by an angel before birth, so that we cannot speak of our pre-birth divine origins. We may come from inspired and sacred origins, yet when we arrive in this earthly reality we come dumbstruck and needy. Or rather, perhaps it is only that we lack the key, the crucial guide, to unlock our memories and unleash our interior gaze and soulful longing. The truth may be that, rather than to forget, we are in fact here to remember.

Sometimes it is a tragedy or catastrophe that triggers a person to *remember* and to seek answers. On a larger scale, perhaps it is necessary for humanity to reach a crisis point for there to arise within people the collective need and urge for change. From this perspective, we can see that the Wounded Mind needs a collective healing before the world can move on. The atrocities occurring in the world have reached their crisis point. The inhumanity of many of our political systems, and the way we treat our fellow human beings – are these not signs of a collective soul screaming out for healing? In mythological terms, humanity is undergoing a collective near-death experience. The Wounded Mind is that part of us that we collectively experience as we pass through our own underworld. It is the shared shadow of the human race that first must find exterior expression before it can be healed and the virus expunged. We must rid ourselves of this 'alien mind' before we can finish our collective journey.

The human soul – the essential element of being human – seeks for something more, something *beyond*. This need for communion with something greater has largely been fed by the role of religious, and/or spiritual, traditions. However, our human need to live a meaningful life has still not been met by our societies. We have developed our faith, our reason, our mental pursuits; we have established industry and created marvellous technologies – yet we have failed to work on ourselves. We have failed to grow our souls.

Soul-making, as well as taking care of one's soul, are not specifically introverted or monastic spiritual pursuits. We are taught little or nothing about such things. We are told they have no place in a material world, where success matters and introspective 'meditators' give little to the world. The Romantic poet Keats said – 'Call the world if you please, "the vale of Soul-making." Then you will find out the use of the world.' It is now time for 'soul-making' to be re-imagined and reintegrated into our lives. We need not go back to animism or alchemy to find soul-making. We can find it here, in the everyday *Now*. The genuine expression of a truth takes no fixed form. Self-development, or self-refinement if you prefer, is not an ideology or a fixed science. It is a basic human right. The inner life of the human being is an inherent human need. It is time to rebel against the Wounded Mind. Only by calling it out, facing it, and showing it as false, can it be healed.

There is an eternal source of connection and communion with a *metaphysical truth*, and yet the 'alien mind' came along and attempted to sever the connection. The cord cannot be permanently cut, yet it can be hidden from view – or ridiculed and ostracized from public life. In our modern lives we have new ways of seeing the world, the universe, and everything. Yet this 'modern' view has thrown away the transcendental energies of the metaphysical. The transcendental got replaced with the transient as it served the new ideology of our corrupted authoritarian systems. Yet the sublime, sacred power of the human soul never went away. It is time we came back to *ourselves* and took a step upon our vision quest.

The Vision Quest

There have always been potentials for self-awareness operating within humanity. Despite the density of the illusion, the thickness of the veil, and the fierceness of the psychosis, such potentials have always been present. They may only have been hard to find. Throughout the ages, various wisdom teachings have operated within humanity with the aim and intention of permanently raising a person/group/community's consciousness to a 'finer' – or altered

– level of perception. Temporary glimpses of these 'altered perceptions' have fascinated humankind for millennia, stretching as far back as when our human ancestors were cave dwellers. This lineage of what we may call the 'visionary quest' has a long history: including shamanism; spiritual practices; religious ritual; and the inculcation of ecstatic states, etc., both in pre-modern as well as modern cultures. For as long as humanity has existed, it has been experiencing glimpses of other realms, and thereby attempting, through many and various means, to recapture these experiences. There have always been these 'glitches in the matrix', so to speak. At some moments the proponents were more outspoken about these potentials – such as the Gnostics – and were subsequently hunted down by the adherents of the Wounded Mind and systematically eradicated (tortured and killed in most cases). In some instances, people have accidentally and temporarily glimpsed these states through such events as a near-death experience, tragedy, or similar 'shock impacts'.

Similarly, there can be almost 'random' contact achieved with such altered states of consciousness within ordinary life. These contacts have also been glimpsed – in a transitory way – by the use of artificial aids, such as by means of induced intoxication. Yet these glimpses are temporary, though some people attempt to continue to recapture these experiences, perhaps incorrectly believing that it will lead to a permanent state. This activity, and this way of thinking, is often more destructive than good. If there is interference from a person's Wounded Mind, then such experiences are more likely to confuse and misdirect them; sometimes with harmful results.

At our basic level of awareness, there is no perceptible pattern to the flow of events. We have been conditioned into perceiving a particular dominant-reality programme. This, as I have explained throughout the book, is how the collective psychosis operates – it is a specific programme that takes over our minds. We do not have access to objective reality, although there can be moments and instances when glimpses occur. The phenomenon of miracles is an example of this, when the laws of a reality outside of our own intervene/operate within our subjective reality. Likewise, many ancient tales, fables, allegories, and so on, are representations of what we refer to as a 'higher dimension' operating within our own. Such impulses help us, whether we are conscious of it or not, to re-orientate our perception against the indoctrinated programming. What we often take to be reality is in fact only a very thin slice of a much 'bigger picture'.

The visionary quest is an inward one; as such, it requires a dis-ciplined focus. Yet as we have seen, not only do modern societies not cater to such practices, they actively dissuade us from approaching them. That is, the visionary quest – which is a way of gnosis (i.e., direct experience) – is not encouraged or supported. The result of this is that people in general do not see – or *feel* – a need for such a discipline. Modern life keeps us occupied and diverted by other pursuits. The visionary quest toward personal gnosis thus drops away from view – there is seemingly no need for it. Unfortunately, it is often the case that 'shock impacts' are required in order for us to shift our attention away from the 'straight path' of normalized living.

As I alluded to earlier, it could be that modern life requires a crisis point, in its greed-based consumptive lifestyles, for there to arise within people the need for *something else*. It is in such moments of deep reflection that an inner realization may occur: the recognition that common (i.e., consensus) culture does not provide sufficient meaning for our lives. That is, there is the lack of any transcendental, metaphysical impulse. An awareness of such lack often occurs in times when there is a noticeable deterioration in social and cultural systems. Such recognition – or *re-cognition* – is not yet dominant among the majority of our modern so-called 'civilized' nations. Yet we are soon reaching that tipping point. This is perhaps why the Wounded Mind is lashing out so fiercely in recent times. It has a taste of the consequences of its imminent discovery.

For too long we have been absent from the vale of 'soul-making', to again quote the poet Keats. And yet the signs have always been there to guide the way. When our early cave-dwelling ancestors first made their hand-prints upon the walls of their caves, they were signalling to the external world: 'I am here – I exist.' The inner spark of the human being was attempting to be heard – to be imprinted onto the outer life. It was an early stage in the expression of an interiorized human consciousness. In each epoch our consciousness perceives and interprets reality in a particular way. How we experience the reality around us influences our perception of it, and vice-versa. This is why our perceptions have always been a target for direct manipulation – it is our reality-sensing software. The visionary quest is a path of experience that seeks to develop a set of 'perceptive organs' that are beyond the reach of external manipulations. The development of such organs can assist in our conscious evolution.

Humankind has had the possibility for conscious development for many thousands of years. Largely this potential has been woefully overlooked and underused – or veiled from us. The visionary state – to perceive with a finer degree of conscious awareness – is an essential aspect of human life. At times this visionary potential has been referred to as *creative imagination* – hence the deliberate aim of compulsory schooling to dull a child's imagination. A visionary state of awareness, as the term 'creative' imagination implies, is an active one: it acts *upon* the world. Such a form of consciousness actively engages with the physical, material world. It is not an ascetic or monkish affair. Just as the pre-modern shamans acted as doctor/guide/elder for their community, so does the vision quest require of us that we actively use our creative consciousness for the betterment of human society.

As part of the preparation toward the visionary quest, one works with relative states of truth, such as is the case for most of us today. We begin our steps from this perspective of relative truth. The visionary quest is known by various names, some more prominent than others, depending upon the location and the era in which it is operating.

The visionary quest to a deeper self-awareness can begin by a recognition of the following factors: i/ acknowledgement of one's situation and the need for self-development; and ii/ the need for partial detachment from one's social and cultural conditioning and external influences. By recognizing these two factors, a person can make the first step to self-awareness. A gradual de-conditioning of the social personality (the *persona*) helps to develop a detached perspective and to see external impacts for what they are. Only then can a clear view of the Wounded Mind be achieved. Usually, this mental pathogen is invisible to us through our social personality that has been created from layer upon layer of artificial constructions, mental frameworks, and emotional baggage. In order to see and think clearly, we need to methodically de-clutter our social personality. Then, and only then, can a conscious step be taken toward inner freedom and genuine liberty. For awareness of the 'alien mind' – the *wetiko* virus – our pre-existing, conditioned consciousness patterns must first be loosened. That is, the old patterns must become less determined, dogmatic, and fixed. Then, through this space that opens up, new perceptions can emerge. As this process gradually unfolds, it is important that each person stays grounded in the world – in their everyday lives – and doesn't entertain themselves with amusing fantasies or unwarranted intoxications. An important feature of the quest for the self is that it is harmonious, balanced, and not in conflict with our everyday life. The human greatness is not in what it has achieved, nor what it is, but in what it can become.

Chapter Twelve

Seeking a Personal Path

'I am not of the East, nor of the West / Not of the land, not of the sea / Neither of this world, nor of the next / My place is placeless, my trace traceless.'

Rumi

'A person's entire destiny – for good or ill – depends on the thoughts in his heart.'

Rabbi Nachman of Bratslav

What the opening quote by Rumi hints at is that our true dwelling place does not exist in any physical location but is an integral part of a Reality that is placeless. However, as we currently exist in a physical time-space reality, it appears we are faced with a conundrum. Previously, I spoke of how we often feel an urge toward something that is seemingly 'beyond us', and that how we act upon this shapes the pattern of our lives. The inner self recognizes that it is the essential nature of being human to seek for communion with something greater than ourselves. Yet this fundamental need for a meaningful, developmental life has still not been met by our societies. Various wisdom teachings have operated within humanity for millennia, with the aim of impacting and altering our individual, and sometimes collective, level of perception. As I mentioned, there have been many instances of people experiencing altered states through either artificial means, shock incidents, and by other random experiences. Humanity is engaged upon an evolutionary path of consciousness development, which induces such capacities as the creative imagination. Genuine wisdom teachings, regardless of their outer naming, all share basic similar fundamentals. One of these is the necessity to develop an 'integral self' that functions as a balanced vessel for the receiving and assimilation of impacts and finer perceptions.

According to these perennial gnostic traditions, the human being is normally cut off from contact with objective, genuine Reality, and only perceives upon a limited, restricted wavelength. The result of this is that we generally end up seeing secondary effects and considering them as primary. Another aspect shared between the wisdom traditions is that people are generally unable to perceive not only who they really are but also what the truth of their situation is. That is why I have stressed how much we are at the mercy of our psyche, which is critical to the notion of an integral self. This vulnerability – or unawareness – is what allows the collective psychosis, the Wounded Mind, to operate so effectively. Also, the psychosis dominates through establishing linear thought over integral thinking processes. In this way, human perspective is cut off from a much broader spectrum of perceptions. We are, quite literally, trapped within literal, rational thinking patterns – another feature of the magician's trick.

It is for this reason that many ancient teachings include stories, tales, allegories, and similar mediums that serve to stimulate left-right integral brain functioning. This helps to actualize an integral perspective, or consciousness. According to philosopher and linguist Jean Gebser, we have recently shifted from a *mental* period of consciousness (which he associates with the 'decline of the West') towards an *integral* structure of consciousness. This new integral consciousness brings with it a different relationship to space and time. We can perhaps see how this is emerging through our development of global communication technologies that dissolve spatial boundaries. Over recent years, our perception of events has 'gone global' and we now relate to others across the planet regardless of previous space-time restrictions. Integral consciousness will further shift human perceptions from a linear, horizontal model into a more spatial awareness, which has long been the case with the perennial traditions.

The perennial traditions have operated over millennia within a more expansive understanding of reality. They are conversant with a range of perception far beyond the limited zone of regular human perception, which is considered to be restrictive. Their gnostic vision is concerned with experiencing a deeper dimension of reality. It recognizes that there are purposeful correspondences between patterns and processes in the cosmos and events and happenings here upon the Earth. These perennial traditions work with the balance and harmony between that which is transcendent and that which is terrestrial – between the 'above' and the 'below'; between the 'inner' and the 'outer'. Where there is no harmony – no grace – there is no true correspondence. According to the perennial traditions, a system of correspondences links together not only the cosmos with our own earthly existence, but also various dimensions of reality that operate imperceptibly to the undeveloped human being.

The core teaching of the perennial tradition is one of human liberation and development. It is a body of knowledge that lives through humans and is transmitted through humanity and human culture – notions of mysticism, spirituality, and religion are simply its overt forms or vehicles of transmission. And yet the transmission deals with a capacity inherent within humanity and not as something that exists outside of us. This explains why the perennial tradition can be seen as a cultural phenomenon, with a historical lineage, as well as a distinct psychological science. It can also be said that the perennial tradition, and the people who function within it, are engaged in an evolutionary activity. The perennial tradition evolves within people, and by evolving, it helps people to evolve. This activity can be seen to operate through the following stages:

i/   Awareness – of our predicament and our limited perspective;

ii/   Preparation – working upon ourselves and 'walking the path'; and

iii/   Perception – the gaining of objective understanding.

The first stage – Awareness – is concerned with being attentive to our various conditionings and the multiple false personalities we exhibit. Principally, it is about waking up to the mental contagion that is the Wounded Mind. This stage requires focused and sincere self-examination and observation. The second stage – Preparation – deals with developing our capacity to receive. By this is meant that a person is required to 'undress' themselves from the distracting acquisitions of everyday life; such as opinions, useless thoughts, acquired attitudes, etc. It is about activating our liberation from the Wounded Mind. The third stage – Perception – is received according to the capacity of the individual. It is known as Truth – there is no room for belief, or other secondary features. Of this, nothing more can be said.

These above stages, as aspects of the perennial tradition – or the gnostic vision – constitute elements in the path of human development. These aspects have taken various forms, or patterns, throughout the ages and adapt to socio-cultural circumstances. However, at their core they remain consistent, and effective. The genuine perennial tradition operates to refine human consciousness so that it may be liberated from a corrupt mental patterning and gain an integral, finer perception. The perception gained from this 'awakening' is an evolutionary one, and its vista is concerned with the 'long tail' of human development upon this planet. An evolved human being – an *integral human* – is both a necessity as well as an inherent part of our potential. The perennial traditions exist – have *always* existed – in order to serve this purpose. The question, however, has been whether the individual chooses to seek their guidance and to find his or her place in the world.

Understanding our Place in the World

The only genuine freedom is to be found by turning within ourselves. The human being is naturally an imaginative and creative creature. Reality may be harsh and painful, yet it is also the realm of so much wonder and awe. We may live our lives playing in the mud, yet our minds can reach the stars. Our science can reach into the molecule as well as penetrate into the formation of the universe. Our mystics and sages can reach into the pulsating heart of the cosmos. The human being has an inner dimension that needs to be investigated and which, in turn, *is timeless*.

The role of refined imagination upon the personal path is crucial. It is what fuses together that which is above to that which is below. It is also a channel for intuition; and it is through intuition that we get closer to the essential. The inward gaze forever attempts to reveal the role of the human being, and what makes us human. It is about trying to understand our place in the world and our shifting views of the world. What is now essential is hope and trust in humanity, and in the richness and resilience of the human spirit. We are on the cusp of a different world coming into being, and at its centre shall be the human heart and soul. There can be no genuine, lasting future if it is based solely on the exterior life — it must be driven by the values that come from the interior of the human being.

Our technologies have given us the means to communicate across the globe in every moment — yet they have not taught us how to cultivate intuitive thought. Our smart machines and artificial intelligences may continue to advance the means of communication, yet the responsibility is on us to supply the meaningful conversation. As philosopher-mystic Paul Brunton writes,

> A change in thinking is the first way to ensure a change in the world's condition. In changing himself, man takes the first step to changing his environment and in changing his environment he takes the second step towards changing himself. For the first step of self-change must be a mental, not a physical one.[1]

If our attention is focused externally, upon the objects of our experience rather than the consciousness of the experience, then our minds will exist in separation. So too will our place in the world feel one of separation. We need to work on balancing that which attracts our mental and emotional energies with constant self-awareness. Importantly, we need to learn how to step back from what we experience and to filter before allowing it to *enter* within our being. We have to accept the responsibility for how we choose to respond to events.

Everything begins and ends with ourselves — anything other than this is an excuse, no matter how plausible it may seem to us. As creative, imaginative beings we invent and innovate. At the same time, we are masters at inventing our own false stories and imaginings that self-deceive. Many of us convince ourselves it is better to go around walking quickly, as if the destination will arrive quicker. We are uncertain of where we are going, yet the notion of walking quicker gives us a sensation of being better, whatever that may mean. But the fact of the matter may be that we have no idea where we are going, no idea of how to get where we *don't know* we are going, and no idea of what to do if we could ever get to where we *don't know how* to get to. So, the bottom line is — we don't necessarily get to where we're going by moving faster. Would the planets in our solar system get any nearer to the sun if they spun faster? Does the springtime hurry on its way to the next season in order to beat itself — to 'out-spring all springs'? as Alan Watts would say. It is not the speed that counts, which is largely a phenomenon of modern life, but rather our internal focus.

In this regard, we must choose carefully where we wish to put our attention, time, and efforts. After all, when we visit a beautiful garden do we choose to sit by the roses and savour their sweet smell, or to sit amidst the weeds that prick us? It is important to gift ourselves moments of joy, for joy is an infectious energy — and it shares easily too.

It is up to us to take those moments, events, and circumstances that we choose and to engrave them upon our memories and hearts. It is also about choosing what things to forget. Most of the things we encounter or accumulate we would do best to give up or give away. We should only keep the few, thus ensuring the quality and integrity of those things we keep close to us. Here is tale to consider:

> An Arabian legend tells of two friends who were travelling through the desert and at one point they fell into disagreement about the trip whereby one of the friends slaps the other across the face.
>
> The friend who had been slapped said nothing, only wrote in the sand: 'Today my best friend slapped me in the face.'
>
> Both friends continued on their journey and eventually arrived at an oasis where there were baths to refresh themselves. The friend who had been slapped jumped into the large baths, yet soon found

himself starting to drown. The other friend immediately jumped in after him and saved him. After recovering, the first man took a knife and carved on a stone: 'Today my best friend saved my life.'

Intrigued, the friend asked: 'Why is it that after I hurt you, you wrote in the sand and now after saving you, you carve on a stone?'

Smiling, the other friend replied: 'When a good friend offends us, we write in the sand where the wind of forgetfulness and forgiveness will be responsible for clearing it off; on the other hand, when something great happens to us, we burn it into stone in memory of the heart, where no wind in the world can erase it.'

We build up and develop our own interior world by all the small things and moments we choose to engrave upon our heart, spirit, and soul. We can choose those things we wish to line our forward path with.

Choosing our Path

We should not be afraid to talk about things of the spirit; to be present with spirit and to live with it in our everyday moments. After all, the true destiny of the world is to become more spiritualized and not less. As Bob Dylan says, those who are not busy being born are busy dying. We are representatives of the spirit, and so should seek to be present to this, without the urge for external showing-off. There is no need for acting weird or strange – to wear odd clothes or follow customs antagonistic to the culture in which we are living. We may think and feel differently, and have experiences that are beyond the accepted, normal ken. Yet to revert to odd external behaviour only shows that we are unable to internalize and stabilize these experiences and energies. To all purposes, there is nothing wrong in appearing normal to the outside world. By appearing normal we are also walking undetected through the external manifestations of the Wounded Mind. It is our duty to engage with the world whilst holding our own. As the poet Rudyard Kipling wrote in *If* – 'If you can keep your head when all about you are losing theirs and blaming it on you ... Yours is the Earth and everything that's in it.'

To engage with the spirit, we may first have to learn how to be still without being bored. There are already enough active distractions in the world as it is — why add more? People are compelled to seek activities, acts, exercises, and rituals to help them along their own path of development or to ease their boredom. The world offers many of these things, in varying degrees of genuineness, sincerity, and effectiveness. Yet the truth is often closer to home. We are catalysts for our own search for meaning, and each path is walked differently. To begin with, we must learn how to articulate this need. This will then begin the course of one's life that will forever alter what comes after. We are compelled to trust our instincts, our intuition, and to take the appropriate response. We are not here in this life to live like ghosts amongst the phantasms of the world. We did not come here to be hypnotized under the magician's spell. We came here for more than this. It is wise to remember that we always have an internal choice, and this should not force us to surrender into the abyss of mass insanity. Almost everything can be a part of the magician's spell, as first mentioned at the beginning of this book — even a day at the office, as the story goes:

> There is a story which has existed in one form or another for as long as there have been human beings. The style of its telling changes with the time and place in which it is shared. In our day it begins with a very rich man who was the boss of a large company. As well as being rich he was also very mean, both in terms of his money as well as his behaviour toward others. He was so mean that he didn't want to hire supervisors to look after his employees, and instead expected his employees to get on with their jobs and to work all hours of every day. Of course, as is the way of people, the employees would often call in sick, take long breaks, and become distracted at work with chatting on social media with their friends. Eventually, the boss became frustrated that his company was not performing as well as it should. Finally, the mean boss came up with a solution.
>
> He found a magician who, after a little persuasion, was willing to hypnotize his employees. And so, the boss had all his employees hypnotized to believe that what they were doing was of great importance to the world and it gave them also much personal

satisfaction. He also suggested to them that the meagre salary they were receiving was more than enough because they could apply for credit to buy all the things necessary for a comfortable life, such as a new television, a car, the latest phone and other gadgets, etc.

He also suggested to his employees that he was a good boss and that they should work hard for him, and not take any time off because any laziness would be an insult to the world that took care of them. To work hard to the very end of their lives, in fact, was a virtuous quality that made them 'good people'. And finally, for good measure, he decided to suggest to a few of his employees that they were better than the others, and deserved respect from their peers. And to some others he suggested that they needed to prove they were better than the others. In this way, he ensured that there would be enough personal rivalry and friction to keep his employees in competition amongst themselves.

And after that, as you can imagine, the mean boss had very few, if any, problems with his employees. But that didn't stop him from continuing to dislike them!

We must be fearless in committing to the inner path we have chosen, so long as we harm no other. The genuine inner path is a subtle one. At times it can seem as if nothing is happening – as if we are going nowhere. Perhaps the path itself is a search for no-place and no-where. And yet we can rest assured that the inner path is active in each moment, in all times. And the search for this can bring meaning to us as we engage with the modern world. Amidst the distractions and entertainments on offer, it is possible to remain focused with our own internal meaningful satisfaction. And this inner joy brings with it its own sacred moments.

It will do us good to remember that life lies beyond reason and is a sacred thing. And we should allow this sacred presence into our lives, with joy, respect, and even a little humour. After all, just a little bit of joy, respect, and humour can go a long, long way – and we have far to travel. And along the road we can reach for the transcendental connection.

Chapter Thirteen

The Transcendental Connection

'Birds born in a cage think flying is an illness'

Alejandro Jodorowsky

'For eternally and always there is only now, one and the same now; the present is the only thing that has no end.'

Erwin Schrodinger

As I have discussed throughout this book, we all live as part of a larger, mass culture, where populations are large, cities are growing, and conflicts and problems exist globally that affect us locally too. There is no doubt that the psychological implications of this are major, and often overwhelm the individual. At times our problems seem beyond the scope of our ability to cope. The presence and pressures of the Wounded Mind are suffocating. The spread of the mental psychosis – the *wetiko* virus – is palpable and disturbing. Yet we are here to heal. Our role is to heal ourselves; and through ourselves, to heal our human societies. This is admittedly no small task.

As a collective species we live and express the human spirit, its growth and transformation. Our social settings – our communities – are vessels and conduits for the enhancement and expansion of human consciousness. Within our social settings the human spirit likewise strives for wholeness, sovereignty, and freedom of expression. And yet this must inevitably come at a price, for we are delving into the realm of a collective human psyche, which involves 'liberating the shadow, bringing the darkness to light within oneself' – a question of personal freedom and liberty.'[1]

The source for real, lasting, permanent change has always resided within the interior of the human being. Although we humans exist as social creatures, as part of our communities, we also require a certain degree of personal individuation. By developing our individual 'soulful self', we can help others. That is, by developing ourselves, we are better positioned to be of benefit to others. Transformation radiates outwards as well as internally. The contrary to this is becoming a 'mass-minded' person, who is submerged into the general mass movement of society, which fosters dependence, imitation, a lessening of personal vision and insight, and conditioning to a lower level of consciousness. This is the arena for the Wounded Mind to project our mass emotions, frustration, and negative thoughts. This in turn all coalesces to maintain, and sustain, a lower consciousness energy. Projecting our negative conditions onto others may seem to make things better, when in fact it is an unhealthy process for trying to make *ourselves* feel better. This external projection blocks our own connection to the transcendental, the sacred, and halters our own development.

Negative projections often attach themselves to external movements and charge them with great power; something which has long been the bane of history! As historian Stephan Hoeller notes – 'When personal neuroses are compounded into social and political causes, they do not lose their neurotic character; they just grow from personal neuroses into mass neuroses.'[2] We are now compelled, more than ever, to find out what it is to be truly human, and to amplify our humanness. And yet no one walks alone.

No Self is an Island

Whether we like to admit it or not, we need other people. Other people in our lives help to teach us about who we are. Their actions and attitudes are like a mirror that reflects to us not only aspects of human behaviour but also facets of our social conditioning. The Wounded Mind manifests through people, both consciously and unconsciously, and other people can also express our shadow side. By being with other people and observing them, we learn about our own behaviour. No one walks through life alone.

It is said that our most dominant feature as humans, and similarly our most ignored facet, is that when we are speaking about other people, or things, we are really speaking about ourselves.

Because of this blindness, we often need other people in order to project ourselves onto them. And then perhaps, in some moment of clarity, we will gain the insight that our descriptions of others are in fact descriptions of ourselves. It is through our social environment and connections that a light may eventually shine back at us.

Our physical presence in this world is not some isolated island; we are all bridges to one another, built from the pebbles and stones of the material world. And it is through this materiality that we navigate our way. Our physicality is 'of this world' and from its materials we are made. We thus participate in the density of the world; and it is from this situation that obstacles arise that veil us from making a connection with a transcendental source. We are often made to forget that there is a difference between our social self (our personality) and our inner 'essential self'. And in this respect, we hardly know our own minds. That is why we so easily succumb, or give away our minds, to the collective Wounded Mind.

Our societies tell us that we are free individuals to make our own choices, and yet at the same time they make the person an inseparable part of society by applying many levels of conditioning. Within the same breath, they command us to be free whilst commanding us to conform. And this dual bind, or contradictory state, creates not only a psychological confusion but also an illusionary sense of self. We are taught that we are responsible as free agents whilst simultaneously we are managed through social processes. The truth of the matter may be something more distinct – that we have a unique sense of self with a degree of autonomy, whilst at the same time being intrinsically interconnected to every other living thing. We are in a grand communion – no self is an island.

Each one of us is the cosmos looking back at itself. We can go further and say that the cosmos is looking *through us* and we are at the same time looking through the cosmos. It is only when we spend all our time and efforts describing the exterior that we lose this perspective. As I have stressed throughout this book, it is the magician's trick that seeks to distract our attention away from the essential. It is like the tale of the little boy who caught a fly, dissected it, and then wondered where the fly had disappeared to. We have trained ourselves to observe, and 'to know', through separateness rather than wholeness. We observe space and we 'see' emptiness – we do not perceive the energy that enfolds everything and from which matter emerges. It is the same as seeing the ocean waves approach by their crest and troughs, by their rise and fall, and yet we miss out on seeing the ocean. We see only that which we train ourselves to see. We tend to fix our senses so that they perceive only the familiar and that which we already know.

Many of the contradictions that fill our lives are secondary phenomenon that keep the game of life in play. The dualisms and the distinctions – such as good and bad, and I'm right but you are wrong – are not essentials (although we often mistake them to be). The world is full of angels and devils (to use a worn analogy), and the situation is that the angels are winning but have not yet won, and the devils are losing but have not yet lost. And so, the constant interplay keeps the game active and dynamic, and not static. Our reality is similar to this, filled with secondary phenomena that keep the ball rolling and everything in momentum. Yet we often lose ourselves by becoming attached only to these secondary aspects and missing the unity that underlies all. When we adhere to definitions or labels, then we have already created a boundary. By labelling we are creating categories and comparisons that by their nature limits us. True things are beyond such defining categorizations. No wonder so many sages and prophets spoke in parables and riddles. It is the most useful mechanism to deliver the unspeakable.

It is the focus upon the secondary phenomenon that can create the emotional response of boredom. Those people who claim to get bored in life may also claim to find nothing exceptional or fascinating in the human condition. Or, to put it another way, the fact that they are a human being alive at this particular time, within a vast, conscious cosmos, has never astonished them. There is something incomplete in this lack of awe; a lack of sensitive awareness. We may ask ourselves, how can a truly sensitive person not be without metaphysical wonder or the urge to ask fundamental questions about our existence? How can we not realize that despite the madness of the world, we are living in truly remarkable times, and with all the disruption and opportunity that this involves.

The reality is that there are no separate islands, despite the 'evidence' of our senses. We may 'see' things in life as separate, yet this is a perspective that allows material life to function. Upon a deeper, more intrinsic level, all forms – both organic and non-organic – are inherently interconnected. We may look like islands above the surface of the water, yet underneath it is the ocean that connects us all. To recognize this is a question of choice.

Our Choice

As in everything in our lives, we make a choice. When it comes down to basics – which it inevitably must do – then we find that we have a fundamental choice between living a life in Love or living a life in Fear. In other words, if we choose Love then we side with compassion, empathy, acceptance, forgiveness, and tolerance. And if we choose to align with the Fear, then we give ourselves over to control, manipulation, anxiety, and vulnerability – all the expressions of the Wounded Mind.

If we ascribe to a life lived as islands of separation, then inevitably we learn (or are conditioned) to place our trust externally upon a range of institutions; these may range from religious, work/career, social, educational, etc. And if these institutions fail us, then we naturally feel vulnerable, or even betrayed. And yet the truth of the matter is that we betrayed ourselves in the first place by outsourcing our trust. If we live a life relying upon external systems, then we must be prepared to feel distraught should those external systems break-down. In such times of great transition, such as now, these social institutions are themselves very fragile.

It is important that we recognize that much of our everyday life is negotiated between these 'belongings' and similar attachments that we pull and wrap around us, like a protective overcoat. At the same time, we need to recognize that our world of 'belongings' is changing. We have 'belonged' to our nations, our cultures, our religions and belief systems, to our politics, to our teams, our communities, etc. We were largely brought up within our collective belongings that gave us some semblance of a fixed environment. And now many of these collective belongings are breaking apart; they are unravelling. Such belongings and attachments recruited and formed us. Yet they no longer 'belong' to us. They were our bubbles that created our islands – they made us trust in and believe a series of external constructs. This unravelling is revealing that our sense of vulnerability is partly the dismantling of our false assumptions. And further, that our sense of vulnerability is the fear of letting go. It is important to be open to receiving information, even if it is of the disagreeable kind. Yet being open to such information does not mean we should adopt a position of fear. We have to make a choice of not accepting, or adopting, these external items as 'belonging' to us.

In knowing this, we are compelled to seek out those experiences that feel real to us, and which can assist us in developing as human beings. These experiences depend upon us relating with the people who manifest in our lives, for one reason or another. It may not always be pleasant, yet working through our personal relationships is one of the fastest ways of self-development. It is where many of our mental and emotional issues can be worked through and resolved. We are individuals, yet at the same time we are one grand, integral human organism. Somewhere within this organism are the heart-centred experiences that can propel us forward upon our path. After all, the Real is not the construct but the profound personal experience.

To understand love, we need to experience love, not to have it given to us in a text message or written on a Valentine's card. Likewise, that which we call the 'self' is only a construct until we can experience it through the revelation brought about by others. Alone, we are unable to 'see' the self – no more than we can see our own faces. And just as we need a mirror in order to view our face, so too do we need other people in life to be as mirrors to reveal the workings of the Self – for no Self is an island. Each Self is a part of the Whole looking back at It-Self. By recognizing this, we are making the first steps towards our soulful freedom.

Soulful Freedom

In a world full of work, family, and personal commitments, it may seem difficult – and for some almost impossible – to focus upon the notion of one's soul and self-development. Yet it is very necessary that we do so. This focus upon our internal development has also been termed as self-actualization. This is a fairly academic term; maybe a more appropriate term would be self-activation, for the truth is that we do need to get activated.

Based upon the theories of humanistic psychologist Abraham Maslow, a self-actualized person is supposed to embody the following characteristics: they embrace the unknown and the ambiguous; they accept themselves, with all their flaws; they enjoy the journey, and not just the destination; they may be unconventional but they do not seek to shock; they are motivated by growth rather than the satisfaction of needs; they feel themselves to have purpose; they are not troubled by the small things; they express gratitude; they share deep relationships with a few yet feel connected with the whole human race; they are humble; they resist conditioning; and they recognize that they are not perfect.

These are a good set of parameters for decent social behaviour and an all-rounded balanced self. Yet perhaps they were also 'actualized' for a different time, a different world. We can work on ourselves, be motivated by our own growth; yet what we do is not only for ourselves. We have always lived in a fundamentally connected reality – only now are we beginning to see this and realize it for ourselves. The psyche and soul of each individual is deeply woven into the integrated field of the human species. Real values that stimulate real transformation within human societies come from our state of awareness and how we project our consciousness. As C. G. Jung recognized, advances in culture are, psychologically, an extension of human consciousness.

The need today is for as many of us as possible to express 'soulful practices'. The idea that our cultures, our communities, and our societies are objective, autonomous entities is an old moribund way of thinking. Society is the human collective; the culmination of ourselves. Our societies, like the alchemical vessel, are the medium of our transformation. One of the greatest forces keeping us in survival 'tiger mode' is the despairing phenomenon of ignorant mass-mindedness. We need to pull ourselves away from being dragged into the frenetic whirlpool of the Wounded Mind that aims to ply us with goodies and treats to satiate us so that we deny our real internal wishes. Yet things will take their time, as they always do. Social and cultural processes need time to change, and the last thing we should be doing is joining the fray with our emotional outbursts. This is exactly the type of conditioned response that the Wounded Mind expects.

The inner essence of the individual — our soul — is timeless. It understands stability and aims for harmony and cohesion. In truth, we long deeply for harmony, not conflict. Within the material world of shadows and mass psychosis, we need to exercise a great deal of patience, tolerance, and empathy whilst preserving the integrity of our soul. The ageless, perennial striving for mystery, majesty, creativity, and conscious development is anathema to those who wish to preserve the power of the abusive mental pathogen that twists and manipulates our human lives. The survival tiger within us has for far too long lived within an environment of separation, struggle, suppression and segregation. This mode of living has fed our egos until we have come to the point of priding ourselves only on our own 'tiger instincts' and our ability to get to the top. Yet contact with the transcendental elements within life embody compassionate relations, empathy, and connectedness.

The ancient, perennial wisdom traditions recognized that our morality depends upon our state of consciousness. An unconscious person, or a partially conscious person, is not able to express the same level of morality as a more conscious, realized person. What this tells us is that the moral state of our societies depends upon our internal states. Each one of us is a carrier and transmitter of consciousness. As I have explained, this factor has been abused by the Wounded Mind to spread its contagion. Thus, an unconscious humanity is less capable of making real choices, and is more susceptible to social conditioning, propaganda, and manipulations of the mass-mind. Soul growth, or inner knowledge, is not an accidental emergence, but something that first must originate, consciously, within each one of us. It's not a question of 'should' we work to become more conscious as individuals, but rather that we *must*.

When it dawns on people that the transformation of the self is more than an interesting idea – that it is an actual inherent potential and living reality – then real change can begin. Perhaps our greatest ignorance is our unawareness of the potential of our soulful freedom and its power to create outward change. We have lived for a long time in ignorance; worst of all, in ignorance of ourselves. There is more to life than just living in the survival mode of the Wounded Mind. It is time to leave the tiger behind us.

Leaving the Tiger Behind

Everything is changing; everything is in flux. As already mentioned, there is endemic corruption within politics, failing systems, manipulated economies, civil unrest, aggravated warfare and terrorism, issues mass with immigration, and a general sense of disbelief. Welcome to the human jungle where the shadow unconscious of the Wounded Mind overshadows almost everything. Our necessity in these modern times is to preserve our sense of self and inner integrity in the face of vast, often impersonal, social forces that surround us. Sometimes we need to remember that life is like our breath – by holding it, we lose it; and by letting it go we find it. Or, as Alan Watts liked to say – 'The more the fly struggles to get out of the honey, the faster he is stuck.'[3] As I have shown throughout the pages of this book, today's stresses and pressures often drive people to find release in extreme forms, or through self-destructive actions. It is important to recognize and identify our shadows, our wounds. At the same time, this recognition needs to bring us release.

If we have the attitude that we cannot expect much from others, then we shall indeed not gain much. This is how consciousness seems to work in this reality. Our attitudes and state of mind are the guiding force. We must expect and believe in better things, despite the current evidence of our eyes, if we ever wish to find a liberating connection with the transcendental. Our human consciousness is directly connected to what exists physically on our planet; the two go together like hand in glove (as the cliché goes). Our state of consciousness is related to the state of the planet, and vice versa. So, we may ask ourselves – which one *can I change?*

Having a purpose is fundamental in moving beyond our 'tiger survival' and breaking from the wounded mindset. And not just a localized purpose for us, such as getting a good job, although this certainly is an important factor. What I'm talking about is a larger purpose – an altruistic purpose. Because it is the larger purposes that are driving change across this planet now. That is, wanting to do things for creating betterment and positive change, for oneself and for others. Many of us know this – *feel this* – deep within us. We are looking for something yet are unable to find it; it is as if we know we need something but are unable to say exactly what it is. As a human being that is fundamentally and energetically connected to everything in our world, then to find meaning in our lives is about being connected to something that is *beyond* us. That is, to feel we are connected to something that is more than us. We may wish to call this connection by various names, yet the need for deeper connections runs through our whole life. If we look at the patterns throughout human history, we can see that this need for connection has always been our essential quest, whether we consider it as something spiritual or not. What humans have long sought for is the experience of connection to a larger sacred reality.

This has always been the primary task of religion, for *religare* means 'to bind'. What we truly seek, and we should not be hesitant to consider it as spiritual, is a lived sense of connection – and especially to a transcendental source. Each person is compelled to discover their own connection with the sacred, whatever form that may take. This seeking to connect with a larger sacred order – to feel and to know we are not alone but a part of a grander scheme – lives deeply within us, throughout our lives. In fact, we could go as far as to say that it lives and breathes within our cells and is within our very DNA.

What we see in the world around us is that this longing for purpose and connection is finding release through other means. And yet, if we are honest with ourselves, sooner or later we'll have to admit that the denial of this need impoverishes the meaning of our lives. Finding meaning and purpose is central to us and is an inherent human trait. This longing for the transcendental connection is at the core of human development. We have to change our perspectives on how things are, and to experience the fundamental connectivity that forms the basis of life. We need to shift from fragmentation to cohesion and coherence. To put it another way, it is imperative we shift from *paranoia* to *metanoia* — from delusion and instability to a transformative change. This is none other than a spiritual transformation. It is time to admit to ourselves that we are playing games. We are in this game of life, and the game is rigged. The Wounded Mind knows this, yet it attempts to stop us from realizing that life is a game of choices by bombarding us with dissociations, stress, and sometimes misery.

We so badly need to recover our connections with a sacred reality that nourishes us individually and collectively, beyond the limitations of a physical life. We are compelled to connect with the sacred reality of which we are a part. We came here to find our way home. As the Gnostic *Hymn of the Pearl* reminds us, we were sent into life to retrieve the pearl — and yet along the way we lost our mind. Here is a recent retelling:

> In a remote realm of perfection, there was a just monarch who had a wife and a wonderful son and daughter. They all lived together in happiness.
>
> One day the father called his children before him and said:
>
> 'The time has come, as it does for all. You are to go down, an infinite distance, to another land. You shall seek and find and bring back a precious Jewel.'
>
> The travellers were conducted in disguise to a strange land, whose inhabitants almost all lived a dark existence. Such was the effect of this place that the two lost touch with each other, wandering as if asleep.

From time to time they saw phantoms, similitudes of their country and of the Jewel, but such was their condition that these things only increased the depth of their reveries, which they now began to take as reality.

When news of his children's plight reached the king, he sent word by a trusted servant, a wise man:

'Remember your mission, awaken from your dream, and remain together.'

With this message they roused themselves, and with the help of their rescuing guide they dared the monstrous perils which surrounded the Jewel, and by its magic aid returned to their realm of light, there to remain in increased happiness for evermore.[4]

We need to rouse ourselves from the wounded reveries of the mental pathogen that brings us sleep. It is time to recognize, identify, and break free. And then we can be the contact, the channel, for the transcendent.

As the poet Rainer Maria Rilke says, 'we are the bees of the invisible', and so our task as individuals is for each of us to be a channel for the transmutation of the familiar things of this world into the transcendent. And this is what makes us so very human.

Chapter Fourteen

The Human Question

'When I grow old, I want to know I've left something behind.
Not as an artist, but as a human being who loves and cares
and tends and helps other human beings.
To do that is to walk in beauty.'

Mary Morez (a Navajo woman)[*]

'And the Old Ones say:
look outward seriously
look inward intently
look outward carefully
look inward diligently
look outward respectfully
look inward humbly.'

Jack Forbes

As human beings we are in love with beauty. We seek the beautiful, and this gives us joy. But our lives have made everything complicated. We make ourselves complicated. As I said in the previous chapter, life is played around us like a game. This may not sound comfortable, or even correct, to some people. If it's a game, then why is there so much sorrow and pain? This is the perennial question. Yet like a game, we have choices, and we make our moves. And there are players and gameplays going on all around us. As I also said, the game is rigged. One person who knew this well was Alan Watts. He often spoke about how life should not be lived as a fast journey and that existence in the universe should be recognized as being basically playful. Life is more like music, Watts used to say. And we play music — we don't 'work' music. And in music, the end of the composition is not the point of the composition, otherwise all

---

[*] Cited in *Columbus and other Cannibals* by Jack Forbes (p. 192).

conductors would play fast; or some composers would choose only to write the finales. We don't go to concerts just to hear the final chord being played. We don't engage in a dance in order to end it (unless we got tricked into it!). And yet, as Alan Watts was so keen in observing, our social systems condition us into grading our lives. As I discussed in Chapter Four, our schooling compels us into chasing grades and making our quotas and then paying our bills. And we keep believing, hoping, wishing for the 'great thing' in life to come whilst we are rushing through our lives with hardly a notice of what we're leaving behind in our rear-view mirrors. We end up living to retire. And when we retire, we imagine we have 'finally arrived'. And yet, to where? Do we feel any different? We have a small pot of savings and almost no energy. And then we are told to wait it out. Until what? When? The final curtain? Perhaps only when it is too late do we realize that we were cheated all the way down the line. And yet we allowed the Wounded Mind to be *our* mind, and we followed it. We kept racing along in order to keep up or to hold onto what we were told was success. But was it ever 'our' success? Did we miss the whole point?

Being human is about trying to understand the point of it all – and to enjoy it as much as possible along the way. The life we have is where we have arrived at by our own steps, and the choices we made. We should not let 'another mind' make those choices for us. And most of all, we should not allow ourselves to be played for victims. We may be under the sway of other forces, yet only to the point that we are ignorant of them. As I have repeated throughout this book, our power comes through recognizing and identifying those other forces that seek to influence and control our thoughts and actions. The Wounded Mind fears being detected and recognized. We need to optimize our lives by enhancing our perspective and understanding. Ignorance may seem to be a social requirement, yet knowledge, understanding, creativity, and wisdom are the truer imperatives. Despite what appears to the contrary, there is incredible capacity for goodness within the human race.

The majority of people in the world are good people. They wish for peace and not to do harm to others. There are many sympathetic, caring, and courageous people in the world. Unfortunately, our systems are run by the minority and these systems are largely corrupt. And the decent people within these systems become corrupted by association or exposure. The main issue is that most of us do not look after our minds. We don't think it is necessary. We are not aware of the malicious impacts that infiltrate and influence us on an almost daily basis. This unawareness – or ignorance – leaves people open and vulnerable. Many people have become alienated from their own minds. This is where manipulations creep in, such as mob mentality and crowd behaviour. Only a large body of people with 'alienated minds' can become so influenced by political propaganda, consumerist advertising, and social management. Mass psychosis is only possible through a collective mindset that has become alienated from a transcendental source. In this state we are prisoners to the impulses that steer our unconscious. We are susceptible to neuroses and psychic illness. The state of our collective unconscious is no accident. We may believe we have freedom when we do not. The forces of bondage are subtle and often insidious. We need to return to the fundamental recognition of the person as a human being.

Being human is about being simple. Or rather, it is about recognizing the essential things. Yet this is no simple thing to do. We are needing to *get back to ourselves* in so many ways. To begin, we must learn not to take things personally. There are so many ways that life attempts to get us to engage with external strife. It tries to pull us out of ourselves. For example, when we are criticized, or insulted, we tend to lash out. We are conditioned to attack in order to defend. Is not one of our famous aphorisms, 'Attack is the best line of defence'? Sometimes this is phrased as – the best defence is a good offense. Yet long before these catchy phrases got circulated through our systems there was a better truism: turn the other cheek. As Jesus is recorded as saying – 'To one who strikes you on the cheek, offer the other also.' Retaliation feeds the psychosis of the Wounded Mind. This is what it wants; it is what it craves for and feeds off. If we give away our emotional and psychic energy, then we also give away our freedom. The ego must be reined in, yet not abolished. It is through the form of the ego that we can find the realm of the essential self. The ego exists as a signpost that the essential inner self is also there. As Buddhist monk Thich Nhat Hanh says – 'If love exists, there are other things that exist also. There is ignorance, there is violence, there is craving.' These external 'other things' – the violence and the suffering – can be, and are, manipulated and exacerbated. Yet the essential inner self remains as a pure, undiluted and uncorrupted form. We should allow it to speak to us and manifest in our lives. This is the human question.

Morality and meaning only have significance when they come from a genuine source. Otherwise it is a 'projected' form, created from social mores and cultural biases. We are the ultimate touch-stone for our sense of reality. We need to have a clean lens and clear vision. And we should begin from the basics – the simple human things. There is a story which tells of a spiritual seeker who after some time comes upon a spiritual master that she feels is genuine and whom she wishes to learn from. The seeker asks the master if he will accept her as a pupil.

> 'Why do you seek a spiritual path?' asks the teacher.
> 'Because I wish to be a generous and virtuous person; I wish to be balanced, mindful, caring, and to be in the service of humanity. This is my goal', said the seeker.
> 'Well', replied the teacher, 'these are not goals on the spiritual path; these are the very basics of being human which we need before we even begin to learn.'

What we may consider to be 'spiritual' is often none other than necessary human nutrition, a daily requirement for living. Yet like our other nutrition, eating, it has to be correctly integrated into our lives, without making a song and dance about it. And, of course, not forgetting that: 'If you insist on buying poor food, you must be prepared to dislike it at the serving' – as the ancient aphorism goes.

It often feels like we spend our days trying to grasp at life, trying to understand it, with ways that are not adequate. It is like trying to capture the ocean with a bucket. The ocean stands magnificently before us, and yet our modern societies teach us to run through our lives anxiously as if with empty buckets in our hands. Personal fulfilment is not only about accomplishment; it is also a question of what we can give through each of our individual imperfections. Here is a story that helps to illustrate this:

> A man had two large pots, each hung on an end of a pole which he carried across his neck. One of the pots had a crack in it, and while the other pot was perfect and always delivered a full portion of water, at the end of the long walk from the stream to his house the cracked pot arrived only half full.
>
> For a full two years this went on daily, with the man delivering only one and a half pots full of water to his house. Of course, the perfect pot was proud of its accomplishments, feeling accepted and appreciated. But the poor cracked pot was ashamed of its own imperfection, and miserable that it was able to accomplish only half of what it had been made to do. After two years of what it perceived to be a bitter failure, it spoke to the man one day by the stream.
>
> 'I am ashamed of myself, and I want to apologize to you.'
>
> 'Why?' asked the man. 'What are you ashamed of?'
>
> 'I have been able, for these past two years, to deliver only half my load because this crack in my side causes water to leak out all the way back to your house. Because of my flaws, you have to do all of this work, and you don't get full value from your efforts', the pot said.
>
> The man felt sorry for the old cracked pot, and in his compassion he said, 'As we return to my house, I want you to look at the beautiful flowers along the path. It will make you feel better.'
>
> Indeed, as they went up the hill, the old cracked pot took notice of the sun warming the beautiful wild flowers on the side of the path, and this made it feel a little happier. But at the end of the path, it still felt bad because it had leaked out half its load, and so again the pot apologized to the man for its failure.
>
> The man said to the pot, 'Did you notice that there were flowers only on your side of your path, but not on the other pot's side? That's because I have always known about your flaw, and I took advantage

of it. I planted flower seeds on your side of the path, and every day while we walk back from the stream, you've been watering them. For two years I have been able to pick these beautiful flowers to take home to my wife. With you being just the way you are, you have given beauty and meaning to me every day.'

The way we each are can give us beauty and meaning every day despite the ugly expression of the mental psychosis in the world. We are here for healing this, and to transmit finer energies.

In the gnostic Gospel of Thomas it is written that Jesus pronounced: 'There is light within a man of light, and it lights up the whole world. If he does not shine, there is darkness.' Furthermore – 'If you bring forth what is within you, what you bring forth will save you. If you do not bring forth what is within you, what you do not bring forth will destroy you.' The interior experience of gnosis can bring insight, conscious awareness, and experiential knowing onto contemporary issues and their distress. We must bring our inner world into the arena of the physical, material world. Both realms must participate and be in congruence. In order to achieve genuine solutions, each of us must be prepared to change and transform from within, and not just by changing our ideas. We have a responsibility not only to the outer world but also to the inner world – to our individual inner life. We cannot live by the conventions of society alone or from the impacts of our everyday lives. We need sustenance from the source that is beyond all social institutions, and from beyond physical life itself. It is up to each one of us to make enough energy available for self-awareness to break away from a state of unconsciousness. Otherwise we remain trapped within a plethora of shadows and under the influence of the Wounded Mind. Our question should be about how to resist the conditioned conventions of the mass mind. It is about achieving freedom from captivity. We have a freedom of choice, whether we wish for gnosis or not. Our choice is thus twofold: between unconsciousness (mass mind) and lack of freedom; and striving for our personal gnosis and individuation. This is a question of our freedom.

A Question of Human Freedom

Dag Hammarskjold,[*] the Swedish diplomat, wrote in his diary: 'I don't know Who — or What — put the question, I don't know when it was put. I don't even remember answering. But at some moment I did answer *Yes* to Someone — or Something — and from that hour I was certain that existence is meaningful and that, therefore, my life, in self-surrender, had a goal.'[1] Freedom, for Hammarskjold, was about saying 'Yes' to the unknown and ineffable source of trust in oneself.

Similarly, Gnostic thought opposes the sense of meaninglessness in life, and craves for correspondence with the essential. Such meaning cannot be taught or given but must be lived and experienced. The living of such meaning is a mysterious process that is revealed through the poetic and lucid spontaneous connections in life. This is also the power of myth, dreams, and the imagination. Gnosis — the inner intuition — is about recognizing the multiplicity whilst confirming the unity. Gnosticism is about inner revelation; as such, it concerns the human question of freedom to know Truth. It breaks down our cages of conditioning and allows us to see more clearly the situation we are in. This understanding has the power to directly change lives because the presence of the spirit becomes as essential as the necessities of our social lives. From the insecurities and contentions of material dualisms comes the stability of inner security. Human freedom, with genuine conscious awareness, recognizes the need for the social community, but not as an *unconscious community*. The human community needs to come together with a minimum of psychological insight.

When communities and individuals lack psychological insight, they are open and vulnerable to the oppressing impulses of the unconscious. Their unawareness of such forces can bring about emotional, mental, and physical destabilizations. It is a psychological trait that when our minds recognize a repressed force within

---

[*] Hammerskjold was also the second Secretary-General of the United Nations from April 1953 until his death in a plane crash in September 1961.

ourselves, a corresponding expression manifests in our outer, physical world. The source for so many ills resides within us. This is because the psychic or soul reality is real. We are conditioned into thinking that 'psychic' elements or things of the spirit are inferior to the physical things of life because they are non-material. The images we have within us, however, can be just as powerful as those without. As a modern society, we have neglected, or placed as inferior, the power of psychic phenomenon. As a result, we are oppressed by forces that can dominate our own psychic lives. As psychologist Erich Fromm put it:

> The outer chains have simply been put inside of man. The desires and thoughts that the suggestion-apparatus of society fills him with, chain him more thoroughly than outer chains. This is so because man can at least be aware of outer chains but be unaware of inner chains, carrying them with the illusion that he is free. He can try to overthrow the outer chains, but how can he rid himself of chains of whose existence he is unaware?[2]

What we are experiencing today is the moral uncertainty that precedes a new understanding as the old morality enters its death phase. Like caged animals that are suddenly released, they are disorientated until they can get their new bearings and discover their new power. As we each gain awareness to the inner spirit/intuition – our gnosis – we gain a new orientation to the world. We uncage ourselves and find a new freedom. The ultimate human question is in finding this freedom and to make steps towards it.

The first step, as discussed throughout this book, is to recognize and identify the shadows of our unconscious that then manifest as external dominant forces – the mental pathogen. To heal the Wounded Mind, we need to know and accept the presence of the oppressive forces. As the gnostic writer Stephan Hoeller says: 'Suffering accepted, darkness recognized and sorrow understood are great assets to the authentic life of the spirit. Composure, serenity, and authentic psychic strength all arise from the recognition and acceptance of the reality of evil and darkness and not from their denial due to false optimism.'[3] The presence of false optimism is like the presence of false gold. It exists because the real gold exists. The commercialization and consumerism of false optimism has been part of what became known as the 'New Age' phenomenon. Whilst it is important to have a clear focus, concentration, and a grounded mindset, there is danger in the gilded roses distracting us from the alertness of the inner vision. Rose-coloured spectacles are no compensation for the penetrating gaze of Gnostic vision. Again, Hoeller recognizes this point when he writes –

> It is precisely this 'open-eyed alertness' that has been anathema to those, who, as the Gnostics might have expressed it, are under the spell of the demiurge. For is it not to the advantage of these intermediate powers – who, like malicious cosmic-psychological complexes, vampirize the misplaced optimism and enthusiasm of souls – that the harsh realities of being should be ignored? Has it not ever been the custom of the demiurge, so asks the Gnostic, to confine humans in a fool's paradise where childish naivete masquerades as childlike innocence and confidence?[4]

Finally, we may ask ourselves – in the face of all these challenges and the danger of a fool's paradise: What can I do about this?

To this question the remarkable Carl Gustav Jung answered: 'To the constantly reiterated question "What can I do?" I know no other answer except "Become what you have always been," namely, the wholeness which we have lost in the midst of our civilized, conscious existence, a wholeness which we always were without knowing it.'[5] As long as the majority of people expect all problems to be solved outside of themselves, our societies will continue to be dominated by unruly forces. Our human freedom from these forces depends upon people willing to assume the responsibility of consciousness, and to project this inner reality outwards upon an external environment. That is the great perennial task: to become what we have always been, and to show others the way forward through our own individual presence and behaviour. Through our deliberate and conscious presence, we can assist others to become what *they* have always been also. As it was written in the gnostic *Gospel of Truth* almost two thousand years ago –

The day from on high has no night... Say in your heart that it is you who are this perfect day... That it is in you that this light, which does not fail dwells... Speak of the truth with those who seek it, and of the Gnosis with those who in their error have committed sins. You who are the children of the understanding heart... Joy to the man who has discovered himself, and awakened and blessed is he who openeth the minds of the blind.[6]

We are asked to be 'children of the understanding heart' — a call that has rung out over millennia. It is a perennial call and it will always continue to ring out, for those with ears to hear. We are called to transform from 'I *am* what I *have*,' to 'I *am* what I *do*,' to 'I *am* what I *am*.'

This is the answer to the human question. Jung was right when he said that we should become what we have always been — I *am* what I *am*. When we are finally able to heal ourselves from within, then and only then can we heal others and the world without. Everything begins from the source: *I am*.

Notes

Chapter One

1. Serres, Michel. 2015. *Thumbelina*. London: Rowman & Littlefield International, p5.
2. Shah, Idries. 1991. *Wisdom of the Idiots*. London: Octagon Press, p122–23.
3. Delsol, Chantal. 2003. *Icarus Fallen: The Search for Meaning in an Uncertain World*. Wilmington, DE: ISI Books, p197.
4. Postman, Neil. 1985. *Amusing Ourselves to Death: Public Discourse in the Age of Show Business*. New York: Penguin.

Chapter Two

1. Forbes, Jack D. 2008 (rev). *Columbus and other Cannibals*. New York: Seven Stories Press, xvi.
2. ibid., p38.
3. ibid., p37.
4. Jung, C.G. 1960. *Collected Works vol. 8*. New Jersey: Princeton University Press, p112.
5. Cited in Levy, Paul. 2013. *Dispelling Wetiko: Breaking the Curse of Evil*. Berkeley, CA: North Atlantic Books, 69.
6. ibid., 105.
7. Cited in Sabini, Meredith (ed), ed. 2008. *C.G. JUNG on Nature, Technology & Modern Life*. Berkeley, CA: North Atlantic Books, p165.
8. ibid., p132.
9. ibid., p188.
10. Castaneda, Carlos. 1999. *The Active Side of Infinity*. London: Thorsons, p217.
11. ibid., p218.
12. ibid., p219–20.
13. ibid., p220.
14. ibid., p222.
15. ibid., p226.
16. ibid., p228.
17. ibid., p229.
18. ibid., p231.
19. Steiner, R. 2009. *The Incarnation of Ahriman: The Embodiment of Evil on Earth*. Forest Row: Rudolf Steiner Press, p1.
20. ibid., p73.

21. ibid., p40–41.

22. ibid., p109.

Chapter Three

1. Levy, op.cit, p49–50.

2. ibid., p47.

3. Forbes, op.cit., p43.

4. Cited in Levy, op.cit., xvii.

5. Forbes, op.cit., p60.

6. Ouspensky, PD. 1950. *In Search of the Miraculous: Fragments of an Unknown Teaching*. London: Routledge & Kegan Paul, p316.

7. Forbes, op.cit., p188.

8. Cited in Levy, op.cit., p202.

9. Castaneda, Carlos. 1968. *The Teachings of Don Juan: A Yaqui Way of Knowledge*. Oakland, CA: University of California Press, p106.

Chapter Four

1. Harari, Yuval Noah. 2017. *Homo Deus – A Brief History of Tomorrow*. London: Vintage, p45.

2. Greenfield, Susan. 2015. *Mind Change: How Digital Technologies are Leaving their Mark on our Brains*. New York: Random House, p179.

3. Gatto, John Taylor. 2010. *Weapons of Mass Instruction: A Schoolteacher's Journey Through the Dark World of Compulsory Schooling*. BC, Canada: New Society Publishers, xvi.

4. ibid., xvii.

5. ibid., xxi.

5. ibid., p13.

6. ibid., p6.

7. ibid., p9–10.

8. Greenfield, Susan. 2015. *Mind Change: How Digital Technologies are Leaving their Mark on our Brains*. New York: Random House, p233.

9. ibid., p240.

10. Gatto, op.cit., p99.

11. ibid., p64.

12. Serres, op.cit., p5.

13. Greenfield, op.cit., p190.

14. ibid., p230.

15. ibid., p19.

16. Rheenen, Erik Van, '12 Predictions Isaac Asimov Made About 2014 in 1964', January 2, 2014 – http://mentalfloss.com/article/54343/12-predictions-isaac-asimov-made-about-2014-1964 (accessed 7th march 2018).

Chapter Five

1. Brunton, Paul. 1974 (1952). *The Spiritual Crisis of Man.* London: Rider & Company, p7.
2. ibid., p17.
3. Delsol, op.cit., p25.
4. ibid., p190.
5. Levy, op.cit., p17.
6. Ingerman, Sandra. 2010. *Soul Retrieval: Mending the Fragmented Self.* New York: HarperOne, p112.
7. ibid., p90.
8. ibid., p22.

Chapter Six

1. Lipovetsky, Gilles. 2005. *Hypermodern Times.* Cambridge: Polity Press, p30.
2. ibid., p33.
3. ibid., p12.
4. Sabini, op.cit., p127.
5. ibid., p169.

Chapter Seven

1. Postman, op.cit., p106.
2. Lasch, Christopher. 1991. *The Culture of Narcissism: American Life in An Age of Diminishing Expectations.* New York: W.W. Norton & Company, p33.
3. ibid., p51.
4. Bauman, Zygmunt; Lyon, David. 2013. *Liquid Surveillance.* Cambridge: Polity Press.
5. Eco, Umberto. 2017. *Chronicles of a Liquid Society.* London: Harvill Secker, p28.
6. ibid., p27.
7. Boorstin, Daniel J. 1961/2012. *The Image: A Guide to Pseudo-Events in America.* New York: Vintage, p61.
8. Eco, op.cit., p2.
9. Boorstin, op.cit., p260.
10. Rojek, Chris. 2013. *Event Power: How Global Events Manage & Manipulate.* Thousand Oaks, CA: Sage Publications.

Chapter Eight

1. Bauman, Zygmunt; Mauro, Ezio. 2016. *Babel.* Cambridge: Polity Press, p125.
2. See https://www.forbes.com/sites/bernardmarr/2017/09/05/how-quantum-computers-will-revolutionize-artificial-intelligence-machine-learning-and-big-data/

3. Bauman and Ezio, op.cit., p12.
4. ibid., p43.

Chapter Nine

1. Bauman, Zygmunt. 2006. *Liquid Fear.* Cambridge: Polity Press, p5.
2. ibid., p6.
3. Fromm, Erich. 1960. *The Fear of Freedom.* London: Routledge & Kegan Paul, p101.
4. Bauman, op. cit., p146.
5. ibid., p158.
6. ibid., p149.
7. ibid., p79–80.
8. Bauman and Lyon, op. cit., p42.
9. Bauman, op. cit., p176.
10. Bauman and Lyon, op. cit., p104.
11. Forbes, op. cit., p68.
12. Fromm, op. cit., p177.

Chapter Ten

1. Bennett, J.G. 1989. *Is There 'Life' on Earth? – An Introduction to Gurdjieff.* Santa Fe, NM: Bennett Books, p31.
2. ibid, p32.
3. Hoeller, Stephan A. 2014. *The Gnostic Jung and the Seven Sermons to the Dead.* Wheaton, IL: Quest Books, p114.
4. ibid., p113.
5. Brunton, op. cit., p74.
6. ibid., p42.

Chapter Twelve

1. Brunton, op. cit., p64

Chapter Thirteen

1. Hoeller, op. cit., p14.
2. ibid., p23.
3. Watts, Alan. 1979 (1951). *The Wisdom of Insecurity.* London: Rider, p104.
4. Shah, I. 1971. *Thinkers of the East.* London: Jonathan Cape, p123.

Chapter Fourteen

1. Hammarskjold, Dag. 1964. *Markings.* New York: Alfred A. Knopf, p169.
2. Fromm, Erich. 1993. *The Art of Being.* London: Constable, p7.

3. Hoeller, Stephan A. 2014. *The Gnostic Jung and the Seven Sermons to the Dead.* Wheaton, IL: Quest Books, p198.

4. ibid.

5. ibid., p215.

6. ibid., p216–7.

Suggested Reading

Brunton, Paul. 1974 (1952). *The Spiritual Crisis of Man*. London: Rider & Company

Castaneda, Carlos. 1999. *The Active Side of Infinity*. London: Thorsons

Dick, Philip K. 2001. *Valis*. London: Gollancz

Forbes, Jack D. 2008 (rev). *Columbus and other Cannibals*. New York: Seven Stories

Fromm, Erich. 1960. *The Fear of Freedom*. London: Routledge & Kegan Paul

Fromm, Erich. 1993. *The Art of Being*. London: Constable

Hoeller, Stephan A. 1992. *Freedom: Alchemy for a Voluntary Society*. Wheaton, IL: Quest Books

Hoeller, Stephan A. 2014. *The Gnostic Jung and the Seven Sermons to the Dead*. Wheaton, IL: Quest Books

Lacarrière, Jacques. 1977. *The Gnostics*. London: Peter Owen

Lachman, Gary. 2003. *A Secret History of Consciousness*. Great Barrington, MA: Lindisfarne Books

Lash, John Lamb. 2006. *Not In His Image*. Vermont: Chelsea Green Publishing

Lessing, Doris. 1987. *Prisons we Choose to Live Inside*. London: HarperCollins

Ornstein, Robert. 1996. *The Mind Field*. Cambridge, MA: Malor Books

Scott, Ernest. 1985. *The People of the Secret*. London: Octagon Press

Shah, I. 1971. *Thinkers of the East*. London: Jonathan Cape

Shah, Idries. 1991. *Wisdom of the Idiots*. London: Octagon Press

Skolimowski, Henryk. 1993. *A Sacred Place to Dwell: Living with Reverence Upon the Earth*. Shaftesbury, Dorset: Element

Steiner, R. 2009. *The Incarnation of Ahriman: The Embodiment of Evil on Earth*. Forest Row: Rudolf Steiner Press

Watts, Alan. 2017. *Out of Your Mind: Tricksters, Interdependence, and the Cosmic Game of Hide-and-Seek*. Boulder, CO

Winn, Denise. 2017. *The Manipulated Mind*. Cambridge, MA: Malor Books

Books to challenge  *your perception of reality*

A message from Clairview

We are an independent publishing company with a focus on cutting-edge, non-fiction books. Our innovative list covers current affairs and politics, health, the arts, history, science and spirituality. But regardless of subject, our books have a common link: they all question conventional thinking, dogmas and received wisdom.

Despite being a small company, our list features some big names, such as Booker Prize winner Ben Okri, literary giant Gore Vidal, world leader Mikhail Gorbachev, modern artist Joseph Beuys and natural childbirth pioneer Michel Odent.

So, check out our full catalogue online at
www.clairviewbooks.com
and join our emailing list for news on new titles.

office@clairviewbooks.com

CLAIRVIEW